Titles in the series

www.amazingstoriesbooks.com

LATE-BREAKING
AMAZING STORIES™

MOST WANTED
TERRORISTS

Profiles of the world's most dangerous people

by Stan Sauerwein

Altitude Publishing

PUBLISHED BY ALTITUDE PUBLISHING LTD.
1500 Railway Avenue, Canmore, Alberta T1W 1P6
www.amazingstoriesbooks.com
1-800-957-6888

In order to make this book as universal as possible, all currency
is shown in U.S. dollars.

Publisher	Stephen Hutchings
Associate Publisher	Kara Turner
Editors	Gayl Veinotte and Frances Purslow
Charts	Scott Dutton

We acknowledge the financial support of the Government
of Canada through the Book Publishing Industry Development
Program (BPIDP) for our publishing activities.

ALTITUDE GREENTREE PROGRAM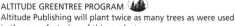
Altitude Publishing will plant twice as many trees as were used
in the manufacturing of this product.

Cataloging in Publication Data
Sauerwein, Stan, 1952-
    Most wanted terrorists / Stan Sauerwein.

(Late breaking amazing stories)
Includes bibliographical references.
ISBN 1-55439-520-8 (Canadian mass market edition)

    1. Terrorists--Biography. 2. Terrorism. I. Title.
II. Series.

HV6431.S29 2006   303.6'25'0922   C2006-900172-3

Printed and bound in Canada by Friesens
2 4 6 8 9 7 5 3

"Kill one Osama, 100 other Osamas will take his place."

Wa'il Jalaidan, one of the founders of al-Qaeda

CONTENTS

An evidence exhibit, showing part of an explosive
device during the trial of Algerian Ahmed Ressam.
Ressam was found guilty of nine federal charges in
April 2001, including an act of terrorism transcending
a national boundary and bringing a car loaded with
explosives into the United States.
(AP Photo/HO, U.S. Govt.)

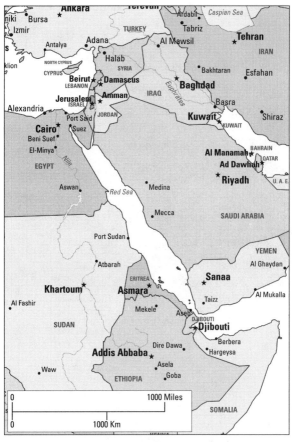

A map showing the Middle East

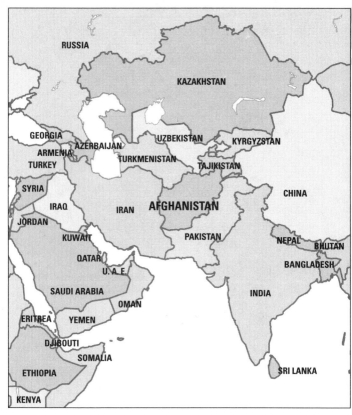

A map showing the location of Afghanistan
and surrounding countries

Most Wanted Terrorists

MURDER OF U.S. NATIONALS OUTSIDE THE UNITED STATES;
CONSPIRACY TO MURDER U.S. NATIONALS OUTSIDE THE UNITED STATES;
ATTACK ON A FEDERAL FACILITY RESULTING IN DEATH

USAMA BIN LADEN

Aliases: Usama Bin Muhammad Bin Ladin, Shaykh Usama Bin Ladin, the Prince, the Emir, Abu Abdallah, Mujahid Shaykh, Hajj, the Director

DESCRIPTION

Date of Birth Used:	1957	**Hair:**	Brown
Place of Birth:	Saudi Arabia	**Eyes:**	Brown
Height:	6'4" to 6'6"	**Sex:**	Male
Weight:	Approximately 160 pounds	**Complexion:**	Olive
Build:	Thin	**Citizenship:**	Saudi Arabian
Language:	Arabic (probably Pashtu)		
Scars and Marks:	None known		
Remarks:	Bin Laden is believed to be in Afghanistan. He is left-handed and walks with a cane.		

CAUTION

USAMA BIN LADEN IS WANTED IN CONNECTION WITH THE AUGUST 7, 1998, BOMBINGS OF THE UNITED STATES EMBASSIES IN DAR ES SALAAM, TANZANIA, AND NAIROBI, KENYA. THESE ATTACKS KILLED OVER 200 PEOPLE. IN ADDITION, BIN LADEN IS A SUSPECT IN OTHER TERRORIST ATTACKS THROUGHOUT THE WORLD.

REWARD

The Rewards For Justice Program, United States Department of State, is offering a reward of up to $5 million for information leading directly to the apprehension or conviction of Usama Bin Laden. An additional $2 million is being offered through a program developed and funded by the Airline Pilots Association and the Air Transport Association.

SHOULD BE CONSIDERED ARMED AND DANGEROUS

IF YOU HAVE ANY INFORMATION CONCERNING THIS PERSON, PLEASE CONTACT YOUR LOCAL FBI OFFICE OR THE NEAREST AMERICAN EMBASSY OR CONSULATE.

www.fbi.gov

October 2001

Most Wanted Terrorist poster of Osama bin Laden
released by the FBI in October 2001.
(AP Photo/FBI)

ABU MUSAB AL-ZARQAWI

BORN: OCTOBER 30, 1966

PLACE OF BIRTH: ZARQA, JORDAN

ALIAS: AHMAD FADIL NAZIL AL-KHALAYILAH/
KHALAILAH (BIRTH NAME), ABU AHMAD,
ABU MUHAMMAD, SAKR ABU SUWAYD,

ALSO SPELLED: ABU MUSUB, ABU MOSAAB
AL ZARKOI, ABU MESA'AB AL-ZARQAWI. SOMETIMES
REFERRED TO AS A "SHEIKH"

CURRENT WHEREABOUTS: DEAD

CHAPTER 1

Abu Musab al-Zarqawi

At 10:15 Eastern Standard Time on Wednesday, June 7, 2006, one of the most wanted terrorists in the world uttered his last prayer to Allah. Abu Musab al-Zarqawi was the shadowy al-Qaeda leader in Iraq blamed for spectacular bombings, assassinations, and the cold-blooded beheading of foreign hostages. He died with seven others, including spiritual adviser Sheikh Abd-al-Rahman, when U.S.

F-16 fighter jets dropped two 500-pound (226 kg) bombs on an isolated safe house about five miles (8 km) north of the tiny village of Baquba. Al-Zarqawi's location, it was claimed, had been divulged to U.S./Iraqi forces by residents in the area.

The 39-year-old Al-Zarqawi had been called the Prince of al-Qaeda in Iraq by Osama bin Laden. His death was quickly called "delivered justice" by U.S. President George W. Bush.

Al-Zarqawi first appeared in Iraq as the alleged leader of the Tawhid and Jihad insurgents and apparently merged the groups with Osama bin Laden's al-Qaeda network in late 2004. He inspired a seemingly endless supply of militants across the Arab world. Terrorism experts believed there was no other leader in Iraq who could match his ruthlessness.

On news of al-Zarqawi's death, Iraqi prime minister Nouri Maliki vowed the killing would continue. "We will carry on, on the same path until the end of the road, by killing all the terrorists," he warned insurgents.

In 2004, when the world viewed in horror the unforgettable images of foreign hostages being beheaded by the Tawhid and Jihad, al-Zarqawi became linked with Iraq's insurgency. Many of the bloodiest bomb attacks against Iraq's government and security forces in 2005 have been blamed on al-Zarqawi's group. Al-Zarqawi's unrelenting attacks on the Shias in Iraq had been alienating many people, including a growing number of Sunni Muslims who have been his strongest backers, as well as al-Qaeda leaders who had begun to worry about the impact his indiscriminate attacks were having on their support among insurgents. In a letter of uncertain origin released by U.S. forces in 2005, it was alleged that Ayman al-Zawahiri, bin Laden's deputy, cautioned al-Zarqawi. Experts suspected the chiding he received may have prompted al-Zarqawi to exploit his foreign connections and export his terror to North America and Europe.

A rival to bin Laden?

In the center of the U.S. military's Iraq war zone, al-Zarqawi was a well-sought target. The military claimed to have injured al-Zarqawi once in a 2005 assault—apparently confirmed by statements released by al-Qaeda—but he seemed untouchable. A $25-million bounty, the same amount offered for bin Laden, revealed that the U.S. military ranked the terrorist as an equal to the infamous al-Qaeda leader himself.

In fact, correctly or not, al-Zarqawi was used as one of the reasons to justify a U.S. attack on Iraq. In the drum beating prior to the war in February 2003, then U.S. Secretary of State Colin Powell told the United Nations that al-Zarqawi had sought refuge in Baghdad. It was, Powell claimed, a sure sign that Saddam Hussein was actively courting al-Qaeda. Terrorism analysts argued the veracity of that assumption, however, pointing to what had been an evident rivalry between al-Zarqawi and bin Laden for years.

Both men were among the deluge of Arabs

who flooded Afghanistan in the 1980s to participate in the jihad against the Soviet occupa-
tion. While bin Laden's background was that of
a pampered millionaire, al-Zarqawi came from
much humbler beginnings. As a youth in Jordan,
al-Zarqawi had apparently been a petty hood-
lum, barely literate, and prone to flashpoint
violence because of a quick temper. The training and experience he gathered while fighting
in Afghanistan focused on a radical Islamist
agenda once the Soviets were defeated and al-
Zarqawi returned to Jordan.

He applied that agenda in a conspiracy to
overthrow the Jordanian monarchy and establish an Islamic caliphate, for which he was pun-
ished with seven years in a Jordanian prison.
Not long after his release from jail, al-Zarqawi
apparently fled to Europe. While reportedly in
hiding there, he was tried in absentia for plotting attacks on U.S. and Israeli tourists. He was
sentenced to death, should he ever be captured
or return to Jordan.

He obviously had no intentions of doing so. Instead, while in Europe, al-Zarqawi had been trying to build his own terrorist organization to rival al-Qaeda, according to German security forces. When a militant cell was uncovered in Germany, with al-Zarqawi as its alleged leader, the Germans claimed a militant schism seemed to exist between al-Zarqawi and bin Laden. The cell members who were interrogated claimed their group had been established expressly for Jordanians who did not want to join al-Qaeda. That provided a conflicting view to Colin Powell's assessment.

His own training camps

It also seemed al-Zarqawi eschewed al-Qaeda's training methods. It was believed he ventured out of Europe and back to the Middle East where, in the city of Herat near the Afghanistan border with Iran, he set up his own training camp. Supposedly, the students he attracted to his movement were instructed in the manufacture and use of poison gases.

There were conflicting reports about what happened next for al-Zarqawi. Perhaps he renewed his acquaintance with al-Qaeda and he began to integrate Tawhid and Jihad with al-Qaeda at that point. U.S. officials claimed that a missile strike on his Afghanistan base in 2001, in which he reportedly lost a leg, was the reason why he moved into Iraq. There was also another possibility. Some experts believed that, at the behest of al-Qaeda's leadership, he moved into Iraq to establish links with Ansar al-Islam—a group of Kurdish Islamists from the north of the country.

Al-Zarqawi was blamed for murder, as early as October 2002, when U.S. aid official Laurence Foley was assassinated in Amman. Just a few months later, in 2003, al-Zarqawi was also named as the key planner in a series of lethal bombings that stretched from Casablanca to Istanbul. However, it was in Iraq that he became the most active, and Shia Muslims were

AL-ZARQAWI ATTACKS

Oct 28, 2002: Diplomat Laurence Foley killed in Jordan
Aug 19, 2003: Bombing of UN office in Baghdad
Aug 29, 2003: Bombing of Najaf shrine killing Shia cleric Muhammad Baqr Hakim
March 2, 2004: Attack on Shia mosques
May 11, 2004: Nick Berg beheaded
Sept 14, 2004: Car bomb targeting police recruits in Baghdad
Dec 19, 2004: Car bombs in Najaf and Karbala
Aug 19, 2005: Rocket attack in Jordan on Israeli and U.S. Navy targets
Nov 9, 2005: Triple attack on hotels in Amman

to be his primary target. A letter allegedly intercepted by the Americans in February 2004 seemed to support that claim. In it, the terrorist promoted his scheme to ignite sectarian violence as a way to undermine the U.S. military presence in Iraq, and he took credit for 25 successful attacks.

The U.S. strategists saw al-Zarqawi as one of the biggest obstacles to democratic progress in Iraq, and because of it, he was among their most dangerous enemies. In November 2005, after three hotel bombings in Amman, Jordan, killed 56 people, most prominently those attending a Muslim wedding, al-Zarqawi came as close as he ever had to an apology. Al-Qaeda in

Iraq had already claimed responsibility for the blasts in the Days Inn Hotel, the Radisson SAS, and the Grand Hyatt. Al-Zarqawi said the bombings were not meant to kill Muslims. U.S. and Israeli intelligence agents were to have been the victims. An audiotape was released to the Arab media after as many as 100,000 people, in a show of outrage, marched through Amman for two hours following the bombings. "Al-Zarqawi, you coward, what brought you here?" the marchers shouted. The audio message said, "We ask God to have mercy on the Muslims, who we did not intend to target, even if they were in hotels which are centers of immorality."

In a rash of militant statements that followed news of al-Zarqawi's death, his supporters warned that the deadly attack would incite more violence. On an Islamist web site, al-Zarqawi's deputy Abu Abdulrahman al-Iraqi is alleged to have said, "We herald the martyrdom of our mujahed [warrior] Sheikh Abu Musab al-Zarqawi in Iraq … and we stress that this is an honor to our nation."

RAMZI YOUSEF

PLACE OF BIRTH:
BALUCHISTAN PROVINCE OF PAKISTAN

BIRTH NAME: ABDUL BASIT KARIM

ALIASES: NAJY AWAITA HADDAD, PAUL VIJAY,
ADAM SALI, ADAM ADEL ALI, ADAM
KHAN BALUCH, DOCTOR ADEL SABAH,
DOCTOR RICHARD SMITH

CURRENT WHEREABOUTS: SERVING A LIFE
SENTENCE IN THE UNITED STATES

CHAPTER 2

Ramzi Yousef

amzi Yousef has a gaunt, drawn look in his passport photo. His big ears and bulbous nose give him a distinctive demeanor that has been described as the face of a horse with a beard. But there is intensity in the cold gaze of this Kuwait terrorist. He has the presence of a man with certain pride, a man with an unbending will.

Rashid, as he was known to his friends, became the FBI's most wanted man in 1993 after an attempt to bring down the Twin Towers of the World Trade Center (WTC) with a truck bomb.

Yousef and his small band of helpers began their day early on February 26, 1993. They left a scruffy apartment block at 40 Pamrapo Avenue in New Jersey, just across the Hudson River from Manhattan, at 4 a.m. After stopping to fill the gas tank of a Ford Econoline van they had rented to carry a 1200-pound bomb, Yousef and his accomplices, Mohammad Salameh and Mahmud Abouhalima, traveled in a ragged convoy. Behind the van, trailed a dark blue Lincoln and a red Chevrolet. They traveled through the streets of New Jersey for several hours before stopping at a midtown Manhattan hotel. Yousef wanted to be certain the delivery went as planned, so he called on an old friend, Eyad Ismoil.

The baby-faced Jordanian college student maneuvered the van through the Manhattan traffic, following Yousef's directions to the WTC underground parking garage. Once the van was parked, Yousef lit a 12-minute fuse and then he and Ismoil transferred to the Chevrolet.

His plan had been to topple one of the WTC towers into the other with his explosion, perhaps killing as many as 250,000 people. He'd been inventive with his device, adding bottled hydrogen to his concoction of nitroglycerine to boost the force of the blast. Allegedly, he also added a container of sodium cyanide in hopes that the poisonous fumes would be sucked up through the WTC ventilation pipes and stair-wells, killing Americans as it went. Luckily, his plan to destroy the towers went awry and rather than thousands perishing, six people lost their lives and 1,042 others sustained injury.

Yousef didn't wait to see the results. Moving quickly, he returned to the New Jersey safe house for his belongings and, by the time the New York City fire department was rescuing survivors, he was quietly enjoying the comforts of the Pakistani International Airlines departure lounge at JFK airport, waiting for a flight to Karachi, Pakistan.

Things didn't go as smoothly for his accomplices. Mohammad Salameh had rented the bomb van in his own name on February 23. With a lucky break, the investigators found the van's VIN number amid the debris of the WTC parking garage and were quickly able to identify the vehicle's registration information. Thinking they could confuse authorities, the bombers had claimed the rental vehicle had been stolen two days before the attack from the car park of the Pathmark Plaza Shopping Center.

Salameh needed cash for his escape and, fortuitously for the police, he decided the easiest way to get it was by reclaiming his deposit for the rented truck. Salameh's plan for escape had been to buy a $65 infant's ticket for Royal Jordanian flight 262 to Amman in Jordan. The cash he needed would be used to upgrade that ticket to an adult fare. On his first attempt to claim his refund, Salameh was told he needed the police incident report on the theft. He told the Ryder dealership staff he would get it and return in a few days. By then, the FBI was closing in, and undercover agents were waiting. When he reappeared, he was arrested.

One of the first names of co-conspirators gained from him was Mahmud Abouhalima. By examining ticket manifests, the FBI were able to determine by the middle of the first week after the bombing that Abouhalima had fled New York, destined first to Saudi Arabia and then to his parents' home in Egypt. With the help of Egyptian authorities, Abouhalima was captured. He was also reportedly tortured because of his connections to Islamic militants who were campaigning against the Egyptian government at the time.

By the time he was returned to New York, others were also in custody, including Nidal Ayyad (who had purchased the chemicals for Yousef's bomb) and Ahmed Ajaj. Abdul Yasin was questioned but not arrested, although he was later indicted on charges of plotting the attack with Yousef.

Yousef's name began to repeatedly surface in the rounds of questioning the FBI undertook with neighbors near the gang's safe house, and they realized Yousef was the mastermind behind the attack. Again, by checking airline manifests, the FBI determined that Yousef had left New York on February 26, bound for Pakistan. Yousef used a passport with his real name—Abdul Basit Karim—when he left New York. He flew to Karachi and then to Quetta, where his wife and baby daughter were waiting. The FBI assembled a team of half a dozen agents charged with finding and capturing Yousef and securing his conviction. However, Quetta was the perfect place for Yousef to hide. A city of half a million transient souls just across the Afghanistan border from Kandahar, it is a place of chaos in the Pakistani province of Baluchistan, and Yousef had plenty of friends willing to hide him.

Again, relying on local investigative talent, the FBI called upon one of Pakistan's most senior policemen at the time. Rehman Malik was able to find Yousef's home address in Quetta, and he pounced on the location with a team of officers. Unfortunately, the investigation was a day late. By the time the police arrived in Quetta, Yousef had sneaked away.

Where he went was uncertain, although Pakistani intelligence suspected that a powerful and wealthy Islamic militant named Osama bin Laden had received him and provided refuge in the Bait-Ashuhada (House of Martyrs) hostel.

Yousef had become a bit of a celebrity in Pakistan. He was the militant who had successfully struck at the heart of the Great Satan in Manhattan. He was the warrior Sunni Muslim extremists wanted to emulate. His fame led him to meet with the representatives of a militant Islamic cell in Karachi in July 1993. At that meeting, Yousef was asked to commit murder again, but this time the target was only one person—Benazir Bhutto. Bhutto was a secular candidate for Prime Minister of Pakistan in the elections due to occur that October. Yousef's new sponsors

INCHES FROM CATASTROPHE

According to experts, the fact that Yousef's bomb did not bring down one of the WTC towers was simply a matter of placement. Had the explosive-laden truck on the B2 level been parked a few feet closer to critical support columns, the tower may have collapsed.

As it was, the bomb that exploded at 12:17 p.m. with a detonation velocity of 15,000 feet per second (4.6 km/s), gouged a 98-foot (30 m) wide crater through four sub-levels of reinforced concrete almost 30 inches (76 cm) thick.

Tons of debris were piled on the B6 level floor below the explosion. The detonation allowed 200,000 cubic feet (5,663 m³) of water to flood that level to a depth of 5 feet (1.5 m) and it severely damaged elevator shafts and fresh air plenums, which allowed smoke to quickly enter and rise through the cores of both towers to choke 93 floors.

The blast location knocked out the power plant for the entire complex as well, plunging more than 50,000 people in the Twin Towers into darkness, as they felt their way down soot-filled stairways to safety.

didn't want to take the chance that a pro-western woman might actually achieve the leadership of an Islamic nation. It was later reported that militant Muslims in Pakistan were distributing leaflets that said it was the duty of every faithful Muslim to assassinate Bhutto because she had usurped a man's place in the battle for leadership.

More like a hitman than a terrorist, Yousef was lured by the reportedly large bounty (3 million Pakistani rupees or about $68,000) and he took the contract. He began by recruiting two old friends: Abdul Hakim Murad, a commercial pilot, and Abdul Shakur. Yousef had known them both in Kuwait during his early years. Like his father, their families had also been transplanted from Baluchistan to Kuwait where, as "guest workers," they had held menial jobs for wealthy families. Now, back in Pakistan, both men embraced the struggle of Muslims against the Soviets in Afghanistan. Shakur in particular had taken action.

He had been to Peshawar and found his way to a military camp called Al-Faruq, where he was trained in urban warfare, the warfare style of the Islamic terrorist who funded the camp—Osama bin Laden.

Together, the three men planned Bhutto's assassination, finally determining the best way to kill her was with a remote-controlled bomb hidden near the gate of her home. It was an audacious plan, considering she was a prominent politician living in Karachi's wealthiest district, where security was the tightest.

Yousef had Shakur purchase the necessary equipment and built the bomb. In late July, he and his gang tried to place it in a storm drain, but were interrupted during the process by a curious police patrol. Although their story about lost keys satisfied the officers, when the policemen were gone, Yousef decided to retrieve the device, perhaps fearing the authorities might return. Shakur had purchased an aged Soviet-made detonator for the bomb and, as Yousef struggled to pull it from the drain, the detonator exploded. His hands were injured. Shrapnel nearly blinded him in one eye, and though it was just the detonator that had exploded, he was knocked unconscious.

Fearing for their friend's life, Shakur and Murad rushed Yousef to Karachi's Civil Hospital for emergency care, but they were soon forced to retreat with him in the back of a taxi when medical staff began asking probing questions about how Yousef had received his injuries. Then, they took him to the Aga Khan Hospital and Medical College and there told the medicos that a butane canister had exploded in his face. That story was believed. Yousef spent two days in hospital before disappearing again in the Baluchistan area.

As he recuperated, Yousef also fumed. He was angry his attempt had been botched and he devised a new plan. This time, he would shoot Bhutto with a sniper's rifle. He scouted the location and the timing of his second try, but somehow word of an assassination attempt leaked. Bhutto, showing true courage, understood the danger she was in that day when she mounted a stage surrounded by policemen and gave her speech anyway. Although Yousef was in position for this "kill," the rifle he needed to do the job didn't arrive in time. Bhutto's attempted murder was forestalled again.

Even though Yousef's plans had not yet proved successful, his celebrity had not weakened. Because his supporters still managed to keep him skillfully hidden, the FBI decided to offer inducements in an attempt to entice someone to give up the terrorist for money. They offered a $2 million reward for his capture. They printed posters and ran ads in newspapers in Pakistan, Malaysia, and the Philippines. The FBI even printed 37,000 matchboxes with Yousef's picture and dropped them from airplanes over Baluchistan.

Yousef's farce in Bangkok

On September 14, 1993, Mohammad Salameh, Mahmud Abouhalima, Nidal Ayyad, and Ahmad Ajaj faced a jury in a New York courtroom for the first time. The trial continued until March 4, 1994, when the four men were convicted on

38 charges and each sentenced to 240 years in prison. At about the same time, Yousef flew from Pakistan to Thailand and joined a group of Islamic militants who were living in Bangkok. Yousef had decided to employ his bomb-making skills there in an attack on either the U.S. or Israeli embassy.

Yousef spent several weeks planning his attack and building a one-ton bomb made from plastic explosives, ammonium nitrate, and fuel oil. He had managed, through the force of his personality, to attract a number of zealous young extremists who were willing to help. One rented a van, murdered its driver, and stuffed the body into the lockable trunk. On March 11, 1994, Yousef and his helpers loaded the bomb into the van and chose yet another helper to drive it to the Israeli embassy.

Along the way, however, the young terrorist's nerves subverted the mission. At a busy intersection only a few hundred yards from the embassy, he collided with a motorcyclist and another car. In a panic, he tried to pay off the other drivers with foreign currency, which only angered them further. Their shouting attracted a crowd of rubber-neckers. When police sirens approached, the terrorist panicked and bolted. Police arrived to find the abandoned van with the other vehicles pushed to the side of the road. Without a felon to capture, they seized the van instead and had it towed to an impound depot. Police didn't realize what they had until the van's owner was summoned. When he unlocked the van to check for damage, he found the body of the driver in the trunk and the huge bomb.

Death in Iran

Yousef was becoming more vitriolic in his condemnation for Shiite Muslims. As a Sunni, his hatred for Shiites was exceeded only by what he felt for Americans and Israelis. In 1994, he was approached by representatives of the Iranian extremist group Mujaheddin-e-Khalq Organization (MKO). They hired him for a custom attack on one of the holiest sites for Shiites in Iran—the shrine of Reza. Reza, the great-grand-son of the Prophet Mohammad, had been the eighth Shiite Imam.

Yousef traveled from Baluchistan to Mash-had, the largest city in the northeast province of Khorasan. Little is known about the time it took Yousef to construct his bomb, but he built an easy-to-conceal device estimated to be about ll lbs (5 kg) and probably made of military C-4 explosive. With assistance provided by another tiny cell of zealots, Yousef had the bomb placed in the women's section of the shrine, set to explode on the anniversary of Ashura, the day of mourning for Imam Hussein, Prophet Mohammad's grandson.

The powerful device collapsed a wall, killing 26 women and injuring 200 others. Yousef was now also a Sunni Muslim hero.

The Bojinka Plot
Intelligence sources disagree about why Yousef

left Pakistan for the Philippines, but the most
likely reason is that he moved there at the behest of al-Qaeda to help Abu Sayyaf, a vicious
local Muslim terrorist group. Yousef traveled
to Zamboanga in the southern Philippines for
a period of time, before moving to Manila. In
just two months, he managed to gather 23 men
to help with his next destructive campaign of
terror.

Yousef planned to destroy passenger planes
with a new type of undetectable bomb he'd devised. He came up with the *Bojinka* Plot (Serbo-
Croat for "the explosion"), which was a plan to
destroy several jumbo jets and thereby spread
panic in many places around the world at the
same time. His new device was a bomb made of
nitroglycerine hidden in a contact lens case. It
used cotton wool as a stabilizer, a digital watch
as a timing device, and two batteries that lit bulb
filaments and ignited the nitroglycerine. The
batteries used for the device could be smuggled
aboard the airplanes in the hollowed-out heels

of shoes, which were below the range of most X-ray machines in airports.

The device was tested with a timed explosion in a movie theater and then by Yousef himself on an airplane.

Using an Italian passport that identified him as Armaldo Forlani, Yousef bought a one-way ticket on Philippines Airline from Manilla to Cebu, claiming he was an Italian member of Parliament visiting the country. Halfway through the short flight, Yousef used the washroom and quickly assembled the tiny explosive device he'd labeled the Mark II. After returning to his place on the airplane, he tucked the tiny bomb into the life-vest under his seat. In Cebu, Yousef disembarked, and the airplane continued on its journey to Narita Airport in Tokyo.

Two hours after Yousef disembarked, at precisely 11:43 a.m., the device exploded. It tore away the bottom half of the passenger who had taken over Yousef's old seat and blew a hole in the floor, severing the aileron cables controlling the airplane's flaps. It was only due to the skill and brute force of the pilot that the aircraft was able to land, saving the lives of its 272 passengers and 20 crew.

Uncertain about the reason for the blast, Japanese investigators first thought the explosion had been caused by fireworks. When Yousef read of their quandary, he made an anonymous telephone call to claim responsibility on behalf of the Abu Sayyaf group. He wanted the notoriety of having carried out the first bombing of an aircraft in five years with a device so well constructed only the minutest bits of the bomb's fuse could be found. Chemical traces of nitroglycerine were found, however, which created a new level of concern among anti-terrorism investigators. They knew, as did Yousef, that the explosive liquid was virtually undetectable by airport security.

Fortuitous error

While preparing his explosive concoction for the

next step of his Bojinka Plot, Yousef had an accident. The raw chemicals used in the manufacture are liable to explode, ignite, or release poisonous fumes. As Yousef cooked his explosives in the kitchen of a rented apartment, something went wrong. A small fire began in the cooking area, and poisonous smoke rose from the chemical brew. Yousef and his partner, Murad, opened a window to stop the choking smoke from reaching other parts of the building, but it didn't help. When the fumes found their way into the hallway of the apartment building, the two men comically tried to dissipate it outside their doorway by waving their arms and flapping their coats.

Neighbors, however, had spotted the smoke billowing from the apartment window and alerted building security. When a guard arrived on the scene, he found Yousef and Murad trying to blow the smoke away. They claimed they had been using fireworks indoors and told him not to worry, but he was already in a panic, believing the entire building was about to be destroyed by fire. He forced himself into the apartment and, though the fire was almost out by that time, found the smoke was still thick. Through it he could see lead pipes, bottles, and wires, which immediately made him curious. By the time he turned back to ask the two men what they were doing, they had fled.

The security guard ran after them, reaching the street in time to see Murad climbing into a taxi and Yousef walking away, intently chatting on his cell phone. The guard gave up pursuit of his tenants because fire department vehicles were arriving on the scene, but passed on to police the suspicious nature of what he'd found inside the apartment.

Once the smoke had dissipated enough for police to enter the building, they were astounded by what they discovered. The stock of suspicious material in the apartment included a range of chemicals, disguises, bottles of acid, bomb-making manuals, and four small pipe bombs. But it was the laptop computer they un-covered that riveted their attention.

In a file created by Yousef, saved under the file name Bojinka, they read how five men were planning to place chemical bombs that would be timed to explode simultaneously in 11 U.S. airliners over the Pacific. If the plan had been successfully carried out, as many as 4,000 pas-sengers might have perished and the action would have closed down flying operations around the world. Each of the five men had a code name.

"Mirqas" was to plant a bomb on a United Airlines flight from Manila to Seoul and get off the plane in Seoul. That plane would explode as it flew from Seoul to San Francisco. Mirqas would also plant a bomb on a Delta Airlines flight from Seoul to Taipei, which would be timed to explode when the plane was on its way to Bangkok. Mirqas was to disembark in Taipei and would have by then been onboard a plane for Karachi.

Meanwhile, "Markoa" would place a bomb on the Northwest Airlines flight from Manila to Tokyo. The plane was scheduled to explode on its way to Chicago. By then, Markoa would have already boarded another Northwest flight from Tokyo to Hong Kong and planted a bomb set to explode when that plane was over the Pacific. Markoa however, would get off the plane in Hong Kong and catch another to Singapore and then Karachi.

A bomb placed by "Obaid" on a United Airlines flight from Singapore to Hong Kong would explode when the plane was on its continuation to Los Angeles. Obaid would place another bomb on a United flight from Hong Kong to Singapore, set to explode on its return leg to Hong Kong. Obaid was then to fly directly from Singapore to Pakistan.

"Majbos" was to plant bombs on two United Airlines flights as well.

"Zyed" was to place bombs on three more flights.

Thanks to an informant, Yousef was captured on February 7, 1995, in an Islamabad hotel room. After his extradition to the United States, he faced trial and was sentenced by U.S. District Court Judge Kevin Duffy on January 8, 1998 to life in prison for the WTC bombing. He received another life term for the Bojiinka Plot and for exploding a bomb aboard the Philippine airliner, which killed one passenger. He is incarcerated at the federal "Supermax" prison in Florence, Colorado. On May 16, 1998, Murad was also sentenced to life in prison.

TERRORIST ALERT

SHEIK OMAR ABDEL-RAHMAN

BORN: MAY 3, 1938

POSITION: SPIRITUAL LEADER OF AL-GAMA'A
AL-ISLAMIYYA (ALSO KNOWN AS THE
ISLAMIC GROUP)

CURRENT WHEREABOUTS: SERVING A
LIFE SENTENCE IN THE UNITED STATES

CHAPTER 3

Sheik Omar Abdel-Rahman

everal of the men involved with Yousef had been regular attendees in a make-shift Jersey City mosque where a blind cleric urged his congregation to "... hit hard and kill the enemies of God in every spot, to rid it [the world] of the descendants of apes and pigs fed at the table of Zionism, communism and imperialism."

Sheik Omar Abdel-Rahman had been blind

since he was a baby when, at 10 months of age, diabetes robbed him of his sight. From the mosque above a toy store in Jersey City, he had been building a large congregation of militants for some time prior to the WTC bombing.

The sheik had come to the United States in 1990 after obtaining a visa in spite of accusations against him of fomenting revolt in Egypt and his having been sentenced there in absentia for the death of an Egyptian police officer in 1979. Sheik Omar Abdel-Rahman's involvement with terrorism was a plot to assassinate Egyptian president Anwar Sadat. Abdel-Rahman was the spiritual leader of a radical group calling themselves Jama'at al-Jihad. When asked what the fate should be of a ruler who has ignored the law of God, his reply was simple and blunt: "Death."

Members of the same group assassinated Sadat the next year, and Abdel-Rahman was indicted with them for issuing a fatwa ordering Sadat's murder. He was later acquitted, but has

---

IN HIS OWN WORDS

When *Time* magazine asked Abdel-Rahman how he felt about a car bomb that kills people who just happened to be walking by on the street, he replied that if the action "is taken during wartime and people are hurt and have to face violence, it is an act of exchanging violence."

He has also said: "I send recordings to Cairo in which I call upon my people to attack tourists. I explain to them that we must stop tourism to Egypt. Tourism is a plague. [Western] women come dressed in provocative clothing in order to arouse the believers. Tourists use drugs, they party all night in the clubs and casinos, and feel up the belly dancers. And our people [the Egyptians] their eyes are popping out from envy in trying to imitate the infidel tourists."

---

since expressed no sorrow or remorse over Sadat's assassination. "Sadat was not a Muslim. He made a mockery of Islam and its principles."

Abdel-Rahman is the spiritual leader of Al-Gama'a al-Islamiyya (The Islamic Group). As an Egyptian terrorist organization, Al-Gama'a al-Islamiyya is most widely known for a November 1997 attack at Luxor that killed 58 foreign tourists.

From the time in 1990, when some of Abdel-Rahman's followers were accused of killing Rabbi Meir Kahane, the FBI had been monitoring the sheik. Using Emad Salem, an informant close to him, they were able to uncover a ring of terrorists led by a Sudanese man named Siddig Ibrahim Siddig Ali.

The FBI informant warned authorities about a simultaneous series of bomb plots being planned by the extremists in April 1993. The massive bombing scheme included explosions in the Holland and Lincoln tunnels connecting New Jersey and Manhattan, a bomb on the George Washington Bridge, one near the Statue of Liberty, another in the basement of the United Nations, one at 26 Federal Plaza, and still another in the New York Diamond District. With the FBI informant's help, the terrorist cell rented a warehouse in Queens in mid-May 1993, which the FBI had outfitted with hidden microphones and cameras. On July 23, 1993, while the cell was in the building mixing their diesel fuel and fertilizer bombs in vats, the FBI struck. Sheik Omar Abdel-Rahman was also arrested.

On October 1, 1995, Abdel-Rahman was convicted with nine others for their involvement in a conspiracy to plant bombs at New York landmarks, such as the United Nations building and FBI offices. Abdel-Rahman was also convicted as an accomplice in the World Trade Center bombing and is now serving life imprisonment.

CHIZUO MATSUMOTO

BORN: MARCH 1955

PLACE OF BIRTH: KYUSHU, JAPAN

ALIAS: ASAHARA ASAHARA

CURRENT WHEREABOUTS: DEAD

CHAPTER 4

Chizuo Matsumoto

Born in Kyushu, southern Japan, in 1955, Chizuo Matsumoto began his life disadvantaged. He was afflicted with infantile glaucoma at birth, which robbed him of the sight in his left eye and allowed him only partial vision in the other. But that tragedy helped breed ambition within him.

As the fourth son of a tatami mat weaver, Chizuo had little in the way of luxury as he grew up. His disability caused him to be the brunt of bullying and pranks, until his parents enrolled him in a government-funded school for the blind. From then on, his life began to change. Chubby Chizuo quickly turned the tables in his new environment. Being partly sighted in a school filled with completely blind pupils meant he could become the bully. Chizuo dominated and manipulated his fellow pupils, exacting some form of payment for the slightest favor.

By his high school years, Chizuo was a greedy, young man driven with a desire to be wealthy. He saved his money diligently—accumulating more than $30,000 by the time he graduated—and compensated for his sight deficiencies by studying the martial art of judo, ultimately rising to a black belt.

Chizuo had a master plan for himself. He'd decided his disability and humble origins meant he was born to greatness, and he was going to seize every opportunity fate allowed to better his station in life, along with his bank account.

To promote his rise to greatness, he planned to join Japan's ruling party and, he told anyone foolish enough to listen, would one day become prime minister of Japan. He reasoned a man of such stature would by necessity have a university education, so he set his sights on Japan's most prestigious post-secondary institution. In order to qualify for entrance to Toyko University, he went so far as to enroll in a preparatory school, but Chizuo was not university material. His disability made it virtually impossible for him to achieve the grade levels required to attend.

The truth embittered him. He returned to his family village and there plunged into whatever decadent pursuit he could find that he thought proved he was "all" man—whole, in spite of his poor sight. He showed a violent streak and lashed out at anyone who belittled him, and on one such occasion an argument in a massage parlor concluded with an arrest for assault. For several months afterward, he continued to mope about the village. Eventually, he became restless with the inertia of village life, and returned to Tokyo to find work. He thought his experience of transforming himself from a man pitied for his disability to one of action could be turned into a business of some kind. Not long after his arrival in Tokyo, he met a bright college student named Tomoko and, after a whirlwind courtship, quickly married her. Tomoko believed in Chizuo's dream, so much so in fact, that she convinced her family to invest the funds he required to open a "health clinic."

The Matsumoto Acupuncture Clinic was a success from the day it opened. Chizuo used his "transformation" as the foundation for a long list of dubious treatments and remedies, which he hawked without guilt to gullible customers. All of the "remedies" he sold included a three-month set of acupuncture treatments and yoga exercises, which were sold for the outrageous price of $7,000. His costs were practically nothing. One treatment, for example, was little more than the application of orange peel that had been soaked in alcohol. When he began pushing the limits of his sales by targeting the aged guests of Tokyo's finest hotels, the police stepped and fined him.

However, the fines did nothing to stem the flow of money he accumulated.

And with that wealth, Chizuo began searching for ways he might enhance his reputation as a healer. He studied the occult and the arcane, looking for rituals he could employ. He took to spending long periods in meditation and from them claimed to have gained the ability to "see" fields of energy around people. That psychic insight was all he needed to convince himself he had a profound spiritual gift. To validate it, he sought ways to receive formal training with an established religion. At the time, during the 1980s, Japan was embracing a new religious freedom.

He was intrigued by the Agonshu sect, which attracted followers using modern technology, including their own satellite television station. In 1981, he began training for his admission into the sect. His initiation included periods of daily meditation for 1,000 days, but once he'd completed the ritual, he felt disillusioned being a follower and not a leader. In 1984, he decided to register a company called Aum Inc. Unofficially, it was called the Aum Association of Mountain Wizards and operated out of a one-room office, where Chizuo sold health drinks of questionable value.

A few followers from his previous yoga lessons signed up to the Aum group, but after Chizuo was able to imitate levitation while in a yoga pose and have that publicized in a popular Japanese magazine, the new recruits flooded in by the hundreds. Aum's recruitment promotion was so successful, that Chizuo was able to open several more "schools" across the country and increase his income even more.

This allowed him time to retreat from the world on a regular basis, visiting private hideaways in the mountains and on the beaches across Japan. On one such retreat Chizuo encountered a man claiming to be a seer, who warned him of the coming end of the world. Chizuo took the bait. Upon his return, he insisted that he was finally clear on his spiritual calling. He was going to lead the new race that would survive Armageddon. He insisted that his new name—Asahara Asahara—was more fitting for that role, and he began to wear white robes as a sign of his purity.

He also began to lecture to his growing troop of followers on a daily basis and added personal speaking appearances to his schedule in Japan and other countries. For example, in 1987 he and his entourage visited Dharmsala in the southern Himalayas to receive a personal blessing from the Dalai Lama. The "blessing" was in reality just a photo opportunity, but Chizuo spun the story until it became a personal mission from the Dalai Lama, and his followers believed.

Returning to Japan after his so-called enlightenment in the Himalayas, Chizuo wrote his first book as Asahara. He used it to attract an even broader group of followers, with promises of secret revelations about how anyone could develop spiritual powers including X-ray vision. Remarkably, the books sold well and spawned a popular lecture series for Asahara. Crowds of followers paid $350 each for an opportunity just to be touched on the forehead by the "venerable master."

After several months of continued popularity, Asahara informed his followers that the Aum Association of Mountain Wizards had been decommissioned. In its place, a new worldwide religion was born—Aum Supreme Truth.

The "venerable master" followed that announcement with an appeal to all followers to make cash donations in order to aid the cause, to work at recruiting new members, and to raise even more money. As the Aum Supreme Truth unfolded, it became apparent that Asahara had cobbled together a dog's breakfast of mysticism that included components of Buddhism, Zen, and Hindu teachings. And to it all, Asahara added the Christian prophecy of Armageddon.

His lectures became an eclectic mix of information from the Book of Revelations and medieval prophecy, all focused on predictions of impending doom. The world, Asahara claimed, would end in a nuclear nightmare in the year 2003, and the only survivors would be those spiritually enlightened souls who had adopted the teachings of Aum.

ARMAGEDDON

Asahara claimed to be a reincarnation of the Hindu god Shiva (god of destruction) and promised to lead his followers to salvation when impending Armageddon arrived. The violent nature of the cult and its particular emphasis on Armageddon is significant as the concept of Armageddon (the end of the world) is not a normal tenet of Buddhism or other Eastern religions popular in Japan.

The Japanese responded to Asahara's apocalyptic ravings with donations and an eagerness to participate in any ritual the "venerable master" created. One of the most bizarre was the ritual of blood initiation.

Followers were offered the ultimate spiritual experience by drinking a small amount of Asahara's blood. As many as 30 disciples at a time were treated to small glasses of the master's blood at a cost of $7,000 per dose.

The treatments were offered to the devoted at regular intervals, of course, and other experiential offerings quickly followed. If the blood ritual was too pricey, followers could buy Asahara's bath water for $800 a quart; brew a tea from his beard clippings for only $375 per half inch. They could even buy tap water he was said to have blessed, though no one ever actually witnessed the blessings.

By the end of 1987, Aum had more than 1500 followers in Japan, and soon offices were opened in New York, as well. Followers were urged to donate to Aum in order to "cleanse." To push the growth internationally, Asahara created the "Shambala Plan." For $2,000, followers could gain enlightenment through Asahara's teachings that arrived every month in the mail.

Anyone who donated $2,000 or more to Aum received two gallons of Asahara's bath water as a reward.

The money rolled in. In 1988, Asahara had gathered enough to purchase land and build a live-in headquarters for Aum Supreme Truth near the base of Mount Fuji. The vaunted headquarters was a ramshackle collection of trailers and prefab buildings surrounded by a high fence to form a compound.

For just $2,000 a week, followers were allowed to sleep on bare floors, enjoy a single daily meal of steamed vegetables, and endure endless pitches for more donations to gain Asahara's blessings. Among the many directives Asahara provided were demands for followers to cut their ties with non-believers, including family members, and many blindly did as he commanded. Some donated all their possessions to Aum in order to serve as "nuns" and "monks." In return for their generosity, they were required to swear an oath to Aum and undergo an indoctrination process that included barely life-sustaining diets and sleep deprivation. For any infraction of Asahara's code of conduct, they were punished swiftly and severely. Falling asleep during a lecture, for example, merited confinement in a tiny room without food and bedding. Even so, the youth of Japan seemed to be the most hungry for Asahara's direction. By 1990, 15 percent of Aum followers were under the age of 20.

Despite Aum's anti-social framework, it was granted special taxation concessions, which raised a furor in the Japanese press. Aum was seen as a cult that preyed on the weak-willed and impressionable. But not all followers were such types.

Brilliant scientists also joined Aum, including an astrophysicist named Hideo Murai, who would help create one of the worst terrorism incidents in Japan's history. And there were others too. Seiichi Endo was a genetic engineer with a Ph.D. in molecular biology, who had gained practical experience working in the Viral Research Center within the university medical school. Masami Tsuchiya was an organic chemist, and Fumihiro Joyu had an advanced degree in telecommunications.

The scientists let their imaginations run as wild as their cherished leader's. Murai invented a device he called the "Perfect Salvation Initiation." It was a skullcap with electrodes powered by six-volt batteries that were said to synchronize a user's brain wave pattern with those of Asahara. Mass-produced for all full-time followers for free, others could rent the devices for $7,000 a month or buy them outright for $70,000. Amazingly, the devices sold well and generated millions in profit for Aum.

An "Astral Teleporter" device followed. It was a network of wires that were connected to Asahara's meditation mat and supposedly recorded the master's mantras. These were then purportedly pulsed through the mats of followers allowing them to "clean their astral dimensions."

But marketable products weren't Aum's

only endeavors. Asahara wanted to create an "Astral Hospital and Cosmic Science Institute" as well—the earth's first hospital incorporating medicine "from a higher dimension." Asahara used the facility to update his blood initiation. The Aum scientists "extracted" his DNA from his blood and made it available for ingestion by followers. It was akin to an "uncut" version of Asahara's enlightenment, meaning that the mystic leader no longer had to actually be bled and even better, the cost of the treatment—$7,000— could be maintained at hardly any expense.

When some of the followers discovered that enlightenment was not going to occur as they'd been promised despite repeated ingestion treatments and months of meditation and lectures, they decided to leave the cult.

This prompted the reemergence of the darker, violent side of Asahara's character, hidden since those days in his village when he used judo to prove his manhood. One man who wished to leave the cult was repeatedly immersed in ice-cold water until hypothermia did him in.

When the man's friend Shuji Taguchi learned of the murder, he too decided it was time to leave. In February 1989, he attempted to leave and was forced to undergo "conditioning." Bound, he was aggressively interrogated by other cult members in an attempt to change his mind. Though the conditioning was close to torture, Taguchi wouldn't bend and still wanted out.

Frustrated by his stubborn follower, Asahara called together his inner council, which included Murai and six others. He didn't want the disruptive influence in the compound, but couldn't risk allowing Taguchi to contact the authorities about his friend's death. Asahara made a decision. Taguchi would be allowed a final opportunity to change his mind and if he didn't take it, Murai was to assist his soul to make a journey to a higher plane. When Taguchi again refused to change his mind, his final route to enlightenment was a broken neck.

Murai and his henchmen burned Taguchi's body in a barrel outdoors in the compound. Days later, when Taguchi's relatives inquired after him, they were told he was undergoing training and could not be contacted. They complained and the Japanese media took notice.

The inability of parents to contact their children in Aum had begun to raise concerns in the community at large as well. Parents made requests for police investigation, but were never satisfied, because officials were reticent to harass a religious organization. A few parents sought third-party help, including legal advice.

One lawyer in particular, Tsutsumi Sakamoto, became a persistent thorn in Asahara's side with his demands for the release of young followers. His repeated requests on behalf of parents for "fair and proper access" were met with polite indifference from Aum, so Sakamoto tried a different tactic. He elevated his efforts to a legal challenge of the blood initiation treatments and spoke to the media, claiming fraudulent and unethical practices were occurring at Aum. Since Asahara could not show any scientific studies that proved his blood had any "secret power," public opinion was swayed by Sakamoto, threatening Asahara's popularity.

Asahara consulted his inner circle of henchmen, who said they had a drug that could kill a man in minutes. Asahara gave the order to use it on Sakamoto.

The plan they formulated was simple. Dr. Tomamasa Nakagawa (one of Aum's doctors), Hideo Murai, and a martial arts expert would wait at the train station near Sakamoto's home. When he arrived at the end of his workday, they would kidnap him, administer the drug, and dispose of the body. But on the day the men chose for the attack, Sakamoto didn't arrive. It was a public holiday, and they realized he had probably never left his home. Asahara directed the men to wait until the early hours of the morning and then enter the lawyer's apartment and murder Sakamoto, his wife, and baby boy.

At 3 a.m. the assassins gained entrance. They poisoned the child and bludgeoned the lawyer and his wife with a hammer. The bodies were removed and dumped in three different distant locations without a witness noticing.

When the men returned to the Aum compound, Asahara commended them for their "holy work" and relaxed, certain his pesky legal problems were over.

However, when Sakamoto failed to return to work after the holiday, his partners searched the apartment. It was obvious the Sakamotos had been at home because of the personal belongings they noticed there, but the lawyer and his family were nowhere to be found. Sakamoto's mother did uncover one curious clue, however. On the floor near a cupboard, she found an insignia of Aum Supreme Truth.

The police were summoned, but they didn't believe there was cause for alarm. At the suggestion of foul play by Aum, they in fact suggested an equally likely scenario was that Sakamoto had staged the disappearances in an attempt to implicate Aum. It took 16 days of public pressure by the media before police became actively involved in the case. When they requested an interview with Asahara, however, it was learned he and an entourage had left for Germany days before on a business trip.

Asahara called a press conference in Germany to answer media questions about the disappearance and, when asked about the Aum badge found in Sakamoto's apartment, he calmly stated anyone could have planted it at the scene. Asahara claimed 40,000 had been distributed, although it would later be determined that fewer than 100 had actually been manufactured. Without concrete leads to follow up, however, police interest flagged, and soon after, the media lost interest in the case as well.

An opportunist to the end and bolstered by all the attention, Asahara came up with a bizarre plan. Why not maximize all the public exposure Aum had received? Asahara decided to have a select group of his followers enter a pending national election.

Although the Aum faithful were active and often broke electoral rules with their conduct during the election campaign, none of the cult's candidates, including Asahara, succeeded in gaining a seat in the country's Lower Parliament. That angered Asahara, and he openly spoke of "extreme measures" required to educate the world about the power of Aum.

The beginning of terror

One of Asahara's measures was the creation of an army to fight anyone who opposed his teachings. The guru asked his scientists to create hi-tech weapons that could be used in the coming war. Hideo Murai and Seiichi Endo responded. They set up a laboratory and, after weeks of research, convinced Asahara that Aum could use chemical warfare as a means to demonstrate its power. In particular, they suggested bio-weapons could be effective. They told Asahara that after weeks of tests they had managed to create a virulent form of botulism toxin in their lab and all they needed was some time to figure out how the toxin might be delivered to a target.

Although *Clostridium botulinum*—the basis of botulism—was highly poisonous, the scientists couldn't seem to find the knack of administering it. They'd tried exposing lab rats to the toxin, but noth-

BOTULISM

Botulism is a serious paralytic illness caused by a nerve toxin produced by the bacterium *Clostridium botulinum*.

The classic symptoms of botulism include double or blurred vision, drooping eyelids, slurred speech, difficulty swallowing, dry mouth, and muscle weakness. If untreated, these symptoms may progress to cause paralysis of the arms, legs, trunk, and respiratory muscles, and even death.

ing happened. Even when it was mixed with the rat food and injected, none of the animals died. The scientists determined the botulism toxin was rendered harmless once it was exposed to air, so it had to be delivered another way.

Eventually, they suggested it could be distributed as a spray in liquid form, and Asahara was deliriously happy. He concluded it was time to show the government—all of Japan, in fact—that Aum was a force to be reckoned with.

Asahara ordered that a truck be equipped with a special spraying device and the toxin dispersed across central Tokyo in the area surrounding the Japanese parliament. While that was being organized, Asahara took more than 1,000 followers to the island of Okinawa to await the results. If the majority of Japan's elected government representatives could be murdered in a single act of terrorism, that would put the country in chaos, and Asahara reasoned it would leave room for a new leader to emerge. In his deluded state of mind, he saw that leader as himself.

The spray operation was carried out faultlessly, but fortunately the toxin proved to be ineffective. While disappointed, Asahara didn't feel the effort had been pointless. His island retreat had raised another two million dollars from the sect's faithful. What was needed was a better poison.

While the scientists worked to perfect one, Asahara decided more expertise was required. He believed that the special skills needed could be found in the former Soviet Union. In March 1992, he embarked on a Moscow Tour. As with all of Asahara's efforts, the chance to make money was not overlooked. With plenty of media hype, he arranged speaking engagements, and before long, thousands of people were flocking to hear his ravings about the end of the world. Much like what had happened in Japan, Russians from all social strata joined the sect, including some top government officials, such as Oleg Ivanovich Lobov, chairman of the Russian security council.

Asahara's pilgrimage to Russia allowed him to effectively tap into the Russian scientific community and its plethora of post-Soviet weaponry. To oversee Aum's purchase of weapons, Asahara appointed one of his trusted lieutenants, an engineer named Kiyohide Hayakawa. Asahara told the Aum leadership it was time to militarize in order to kick-start the beginning of Armageddon. He told them he wanted bio-weapons, conventional weapons, and nuclear devices for the impending battle. His favorite scientist, Murai, was charged with producing chemical weapons, which included an old Nazi invention—sarin.

As well as buying firearms, explosives, tanks, and aircraft, Asahara undertook to see that every Aum member received military training. Any former soldiers in the group suddenly became instructors, and Asahara had a special commando unit. Created from the best recruits, they would be responsible for security and intelligence. As if he were a country unto himself, Asahara began to arm Aum. He purchased an ironworks company and stripped it of its tools, moving them to a new building in the Mount Fuji compound. The 47,000-square-foot (4,366 m^2) building was called "Clear Stream Temple," but its real purpose had nothing to do with peace. This temple was to become a manufacturing facility where Aum could make parts for the Russian-designed AK-74 rifle. The AK-74 was an upgraded version of the AK-47, and Asahara's goal was to provide every cult member with a rifle and ammunition by 1995.

To help supply Aum's scientists with equipment and the raw materials they needed to produce large quantities of deadly nerve gas and other biological toxins, Asahara had Aum undertake a massive business expansion.

Aum already had a complicated web of legitimate businesses that had been created to make use of its donation revenue. Through one company—Mahaposya—Aum expanded into nearly every business necessary to sustain the life of its membership.

The company also opened a chain of budget computer stores across the country, which mainly sold American-made computer hardware. The retail concept was so successful, it expanded to over 300 stores by the end of 1993. With residential, commercial, and industrial real estate holdings, plus the regular flow of member donations and Aum's corporate earnings, Aum's financial officers estimated Asahara's wealth to be in excess of a billion dollars.

Even though Asahara preached an austere life of religious devotion, the one he lived was decadent. He surrounded himself in luxury, with a fleet of cars, yachts, and servants, while sect members slaved long hours for meager meals in cramped and often unsanitary conditions. He demanded his scientists create weapons of war with the impatience of a spoiled child.

Once again, the scientists tried to create mass panic. They timed the spraying of a new version of their botulism cocktail throughout central Toyko to coincide with the wedding of Japan's Prince Naruhito. Once again, they failed.

Aum's scientists finally decided a different weapon was required for the arsenal. In late 1993, an eight-story building Aum owned in the east end of Tokyo was converted into a laboratory to produce anthrax.

One cult member, who was a graduate

student in biology, obtained a sample of what he thought to be a deadly strain of anthrax. In actuality, it was a veterinary anthrax vaccine strain that could not cause disease. However, the scientists proceeded to work with the anthrax thinking otherwise, and they cultured the bacteria in large drums. Rather than converting it to a powder, the scientists manufactured the anthrax in a liquid form. They erected a test device on the roof of the laboratory—an industrial sprayer that would extract the anthrax spores from the lab a floor below and spread it over the neighborhood. The machine reportedly ran for at least a day and perhaps as long as several for their test.

It wasn't long before local residents were reporting a disgusting smell in the area. Plants were wilting, pets became ill, and people complained of stomach ailments. However, no one died from contact to anthrax spores.

The police eventually identified the Aum building as the source of the stench, but accepted Asahara's explanation that the smell was a combination of perfume and soybean oil that had been burned to "purify" the building. They took samples of a fluid emanating from a pipe on the building, but investigated the matter no further.

Even with three failures, Asahara wasn't ready to give up. He ordered his scientists to work harder and dispatched a team to Africa with the hope they might be able to procure samples of the dangerous Ebola virus. Other teams were sent to the United States to try to learn more about biological warfare, and Hayakawa went to Russia with a "priority" shopping list. Asahara wanted him to buy an ex-army helicopter, a MiG-29 fighter jet, and a SL-13 Proton rocket launcher, but Hayakawa only succeeded in purchasing the helicopter.

Sarin—the answer

While this activity was underway, the chemists in the Mount Fuji compound continued to work.

Housed in a $10 million lab, it was the chemists who were finally able to report success to their leader. They had been able to produce one of the most deadly nerve toxins known to man— sarin. A single droplet on the skin will kill an adult. Chemist Masami

SARIN

Sarin is an extremely toxic human-made poison classified as a weapon of mass destruction by the United Nations. It attacks the nervous system and can be fatal even at very low concentrations. Sarin is estimated to be more than 500 times as toxic as cyanide.

Tsuchiya reported to his leader that within their computer-controlled laboratory, they could produce 17.6 pints (8.3 L) of liquid sarin at a time, or two tons a day.

Asahara was overjoyed. He ordered the production of a massive 70 tons, which he calculated would be enough of the toxin to kill every living thing on the planet. Within minutes of exposure to sarin in either liquid or gas form, the victim's nose begins to run. This is accompanied by tightening of the chest that develops into violent spasms, followed by vomiting and loss of bladder and bowel control. Death is preceded by convulsions and coma.

The cult tested their sarin on animals at an Australian sheep farm operated by the sect, but Asahara wanted a human trial. He decided to test the toxin on Daisaku Ikeda, the leader of Soka Gakkai, a popular "new religion" in Japan and one Asahara considered a rival to Aum.

Asahara directed his followers to rig a spraying device on a suitable vehicle and use it during a public rally by Ikeda. Their first attempt failed when the sprayer wouldn't operate. Then the sprayer sprang a leak, splashing sarin on one of the testers. Fortunately for him, an antidote was quickly administered.

A legal problem gave Asahara a different opportunity for a human test. Aum was purchasing a food processing concern when the owner learned who the prospective buyer was, and tried to invalidate the sale. A court case resulted, and as the trial ended and the three trial judges retired to consider their verdict, Asahara was told by his legal team that it was highly likely Aum would lose the case. Furious, Asahara ordered his chemists to use sarin to kill the judges.

The team decided to use a large truck, fitted with a sophisticated battery-powered atomizer and 44 pounds (20 kg) of sarin. However, on the day of the attack, a series of timing errors caused the truck to arrive too late at the court building for the judges to be attacked.

Instead, the chemists drove to the heavily populated Matsumoto area where they knew the judges were staying and attempted to spray the sarin. When the device malfunctioned, a deadly cloud of hydrogen chloride was released from the truck. The cloud was so dense that the truck's occupants couldn't see where they were driving. As they tried to correct matters, the winds changed direction. The deadly cloud wafted over the neighborhood away from the judges, killing seven and putting 150 more into hospital with blinding headaches and violent stomach spasms. Despite the failure of the attack from a technical perspective, Asahara was pleased with the result.

Police still didn't consider the Aum group as suspects. Instead, they arrested one of the affected residents after chemicals were found in a storage shed on his property. An anonymous tip finally prompted them to turn their attention to the real perpetrators. In a written note, someone gave police a dire warning:

"Matsumoto was definitely an experiment of sorts. The result of this experiment in an open space: seven dead, over 200 injured. If sarin is released in an enclosed space say, a crowded subway, it is easy to imagine a massive catastrophe." However, even with that warning, the police undertook no proactive efforts to nullify the Aum threat.

The subway attack

The deadly results were all the proof Asahara needed. He decided the time had come to launch his first real attack. He targeted the Tokyo subway system.

Asahara gathered 100 of his most loyal followers and urged them to "fight as one." He predicted that the attack would result in intense police investigation and he would likely be arrested as a suspect, but he assured them that Aum would prevail. The meeting with his followers would be the last speech the guru master would give his cult.

Asahara wanted to use the subway system to strike a massive lethal blow. Tokyo's subway system transports more than 5 million people a day with a precision that is remarkable to witness. By using sarin, the death toll could be enormous. The main target for the attack was Kasumigaseki station and it was coordinated to start in the middle of morning rush hour on March 20, 1995.

Hideo Murai was put in charge. To avoid the equipment failures that had plagued every other mission, Murai came up with a simpler solution. Members would hand-deliver plastic bags filled with sarin to the subway. When in place, the members could puncture the bag with an umbrella equipped with a sharpened tip. As the sarin leaked out, it would infect its victims unseen. Murai selected nine men for the mission.

Several hours before dawn, each man was given a knapsack filled with sarin bags and a supply of antidote pills. Each member was dropped off at a different station to board a train destined for Kasumigaseki station. As their train approached the station, the sect followers were to puncture their packages with the umbrellas and exit the train.

Within seconds of the bags having been punctured, sarin gas fumes spread through each targeted subway carriage. Almost immediately, passengers on the trains began coughing and feeling nauseous. As the trains reached their next stops, several passengers tried to exit their carriages and collapsed on the train platforms. Many were trampled by other commuters trying to flee the sudden plague affecting the train compartments.

It took mere minutes for the surrounding stations to be littered with the dead and dying. Ambulances were rushed to each station, but the emergency responders were unsure what was causing the sudden illness. Over the course of just a few hours, 12 people were listed dead and 5500 others had to be treated for injury. Until military experts called to the scenes established that the commuters had been affected by sarin nerve gas, the "instant plague" was a total mystery.

Once the Aum followers executed their missions, they returned to the Mount Fuji compound, where Asahara happily congratulated them. He paid them for their service to the cause and told everyone to seek a place to hide.

News spread quickly within the Aum community about what had happened. Within the compound, the sect followers were suddenly in a panicked rush to destroy evidence. Chemicals were buried or burned, equipment dismantled or moved, and records destroyed. Hundreds of the followers immediately fled, including Asahara, who escaped in his Rolls Royce. Although the distinctive automobile was followed by police, it managed to elude them, and Asahara stayed untouchable for more than two months.

Shortly after dawn on March 22, more than 1,000 police stormed the Mount Fuji headquarters of Aum Supreme Truth. Many of the police officers wore special chemical warfare suits, prepared for the likelihood that sarin would be found.

Police combed the compound for a week, finding 200 different chemical substances for making sarin in sufficient quantities to kill four million people or more. They uncovered other dangerous chemicals and the equipment necessary to make deadly weapons. As well, searchers found a hospital stocked with exotic drugs, millions of dollars in cash and gold, and several torture cells, some still holding followers who were undergoing "conditioning." However, the police made no arrests.

Aum's legal team countered the police raids with denials of wrongdoing and lawsuits against the city for damages. They claimed that the chemicals were for the manufacture of fertilizer and food products. Via a recorded video statement, Asahara told the world that he and Aum were innocent. He suggested that "the Tokyo subway attack was an attempt by the U.S. military to implicate the cult."

The leaders of the cult became the nation's most wanted criminals. Several sect members continued to act independently, attacking police and even shooting Takaji Kunimatsu (chief of the national police agency) four times with a heavy-caliber revolver as he entered his office.

By early April, the police investigation began to produce results. Some of the sect's leaders were found, and on May 16, 1995, Asahara himself was discovered in hiding in the very compound the police had been searching for months.

Asahara was charged with 23 counts of murder, and he pleaded not guilty on all counts. The trials involving the inner circle of the cult began in 1996. The charges against many of the leaders included murder, attempted murder, kidnapping, manufacture of dangerous drugs, and a score of lesser charges. Some gave full confessions in a bid to avoid the death penalty.

On February 27, 2004, Asahara Asahara, the founder of the AUM Shinrikyo cult was sentenced to death in the Tokyo District Court after being convicted on 13 charges that claimed the lives of 27 victims. The trial was a media circus in Japan, stirring up nationwide interest. Nearly 5,000 people lined up outside the court building, in the hope of getting one of the 38 seats available in the public gallery.

Presiding Judge Shoji Ogawa handed down the trial ruling saying: "The crimes were cruel and inhuman, and his responsibility as the mastermind behind all the cases is extremely grave. He deserves the maximum punishment.

He had dreams of being delivered from earth's bonds and attempted to rule Japan as a king under the pretext of salvaging people. He had a selfish dogma of killing those who he thought were obstructing his bid, and he armed his cult. He threw people in Japan and overseas into terror. It was an unprecedentedly brutal and serious crime."

Judge Ogawa continued his criticism of the accused: "It's impossible to describe the feelings of the victims of his crime. However, the defendant has failed to express an apology, and placed the blame on his followers."

The court found that Asahara Asahara had:
- Masterminded the 13 cases for which he was indicted.
- Ordered the 1989 murder of anti-AUM lawyer Tsutsumi Sakamoto, his wife, and their infant son.
- Ordered the June 1994 sarin gas attack in Matsumoto, Nagano Prefecture, which left seven residents dead.

- Ordered the March 1995 sarin attacks on Tokyo subway trains, which killed 12 passengers and subway workers and sickened thousands of others.
- Sprayed VX gas on three people, killing one of them.
- Masterminded the abduction of a notary in February 1995 in a bid to find the whereabouts of a relative who had escaped from the cult, and fatally injecting him with excessive amounts of anesthesia.
- Prepared to carry out murder by ordering the construction of a sarin plant between 1993 and 1994.
- Ordered the murder of three cult followers.
- Ordered a sarin attack on another anti-cult lawyer in 1994, in an unsuccessful bid to kill him.
- Undertook the illegal production of small firearms in the mid-1990s.

As the judgment was being read out, Asahara smiled, laughed, and yawned. At the end of the four-hour judgment, Judge Ogawa sentenced Asahara to death.

TIMOTHY MCVEIGH

BORN: APRIL 23, 1968

PLACE OF BIRTH: PENDLETON, NEW YORK

CURRENT WHEREABOUTS: DEAD

CHAPTER 5

Timothy McVeigh

Not long after the workday had begun in Oklahoma City on April 19, 1995, a thin, young man parked his yellow Ryder Rental truck outside the Alfred P. Murrah Building. He calmly slid out of the cab, made sure the doors were locked, and then walked away unnoticed.

On that beautiful, sunny morning, nothing seemed amiss until 9:02 a.m., when a 4,000-pound (1,814 kg) bomb ignited in the cargo hold of the truck. The blast was so powerful, it managed to chew through one-third of the seven-story federal building in an instant. This event etched into the nation's psyche a shocking awareness that the United States was vulnerable to terrorism.

The 27-year-old man who delivered the deathblow had managed to get far enough away from the explosion to avoid injury. When the bomb's shock wave traveled through the earth, it was strong enough to lift pedestrians off the ground blocks away. And although everyone else on the street was transfixed by the sudden cloud of smoke and raining debris, the bomber barely broke stride.

Oklahoma Trooper Charlie Hanger was among the hundreds of police soon dispatched to offer aid to the injured, but he never made it to the scene of the blast. Before he could reach the devastation, his order was rescinded, and the dispatcher told him to return to his post in Noble County. Charlie did as he was ordered and headed northward on I-35.

Hanger was alert and tense as he monitored the chatter on his radio. The events in Oklahoma City riveted him, as news of rescue efforts unfolded. Perhaps that is why his attention was caught by a yellow car—the same color as the truck that had exploded. As the beat-up 1977 Mercury Grand Marquis with no license plate crossed his vision about 75 miles (121 km) away from the disaster site, Hanger hit his siren and lights.

He pulled the car over onto the shoulder of the highway, expecting to do no more than ticket the driver for a violation. Hanger watched carefully as a tall, thin young man climbed out of the yellow heap and walked toward his cruiser.

Hanger asked the man if he was aware that his car had no plate. The young man nodded. He told Hanger he'd just bought the vehicle. Hanger was immediately suspicious. He asked the young man if he had insurance and registration or a bill of sale to prove his story. The driver shook his head and said he had none of that as it was being mailed to him, but he had a driver's license and he reached into his pocket for his wallet to offer it up for inspection.

Trooper Hanger tensed immediately. The man's movement had given the policeman a brief glimpse of something, and he drew his weapon. "What's that?" Hanger asked, pointing his sidearm at the driver.

"A Glock," the driver replied calmly.

"Raise your hands and turn around."

The young man did as he was told. While Hanger took away the 9-mm handgun plus an ammo clip and a knife, the driver complained that he had a legal right to be carrying a gun. The Trooper offered no argument. Instead he cuffed the driver, who he now considered a dangerous suspect. He then contacted his dispatcher to run a check on Timothy McVeigh, for both his Michigan license and his permit for the Glock.

"New York permits aren't legal in Oklahoma," he told the man, so McVeigh was guilty of a crime for carrying a concealed weapon. With McVeigh cuffed and secure, Hanger asked for permission to search McVeigh's car.

"Got anything in there you want to tell me about first?" Hanger asked in his patient drawl.

McVeigh shook his head. "Go ahead and search."

In the Mercury, Hanger found only a baseball cap, some tools, and a white envelope. He left everything he found in the car, which he locked. Then Hanger informed the driver that he would be transported to Noble County Jail in Perry, Oklahoma, for processing on possible charges.

As they drove to Perry, Hanger returned his attention to the radio, occasionally glancing at his prisoner in the mirror. He didn't notice that McVeigh had managed to pull a business card from his pocket and drop it in plain view. The card belonged to Dave Paulson, a military supply dealer. It had notes scratched on one side.

McVeigh had planned a little payback for the dealer who had reneged on a deal McVeigh had made to buy dynamite and blasting caps. Expecting to be caught, the bomber had written information on the card that could implicate Paulson in what he'd just done in Oklahoma City. "TNT $5/stick need more" the card read.

In Perry, McVeigh was processed on four misdemeanors: unlawfully carrying a weapon, transporting a loaded firearm in a motor vehicle, failing to display a current license plate, and not having proof of insurance for the vehicle. Everything else about McVeigh seemed in order, and although the charges were minor, he was told he would remain in custody until Judge Danny G. Allen could hear his case. His hearing wouldn't happen for a few days.

The events in Perry police station were calm compared to the frenzy of police activity happening elsewhere across the country. FBI investigators busily tried to generate leads and answers to who had committed the Oklahoma City bombing and why. There was a suspicion that it had been perpetrated by foreign terrorists, and within hours of the attack, eight groups had claimed responsibility. That prompted the CIA, the National Security Agency, the National Counterterrorism Center, and the National Reconnaissance Office to scour data records for information concerning radical Islamic suspects in the United States. More than 100 possible perpetrators were identified, as the FBI focused its effort on Islamic Jihad and tightened an international dragnet to detain any young men traveling alone to the Middle East from the United States.

While McVeigh remained unsuspected in Perry, investigators combed the debris in Oklahoma City for clues. After two days, they finally had some luck: They recovered the axle of the truck they believed was used in the bombing. The axle had a legible vehicle identification number on it. They also found the rear bumper from the same truck with its license plate number still legible. Using the two bits of information, the FBI traced the truck to a Ryder dealership in Junction City, Kansas. A check determined that a man named Robert Kling had rented the vehicle.

With the help of the Ryder Rental agency staff in Junction City, FBI investigators were able to compile a composite drawing of two men. One was an individual who called himself Kling. They had no name for the second man. Canvassing hotels and motels in the area, by that evening they spoke to the manager of the Dreamland Motel. She recognized the face of the man the FBI knew as Kling, but she said his name was McVeigh. At least, that was the name he used when he registered.

The manager also described the car McVeigh was driving. It was an old yellow Marquis, the same color as a large Ryder truck he parked at the motel not long after. She provided the police officers with the address that had been given on the registration—a farm in Decker, Michigan.

A routine check quickly determined a man

named McVeigh, who had the same address on his driver's license, was resting quietly in the Perry police station on unrelated charges. With profound hope that the perpetrator had already been caught, FBI agents immediately headed for Noble County. As McVeigh waited near the courtroom for his hearing, the sheriff in Perry was notified that the FBI was on the way. He was asked to stall McVeigh's release as long as possible.

McVeigh expected to be facing a judge, but instead officers came into the waiting area and shrugged their shoulders. "The judge isn't ready for you," they told McVeigh, as they led him back to his cell. "You'll have to wait a little longer." Worried that McVeigh might contact a lawyer to effect an immediate release, someone disconnected the pay telephone in the cell. McVeigh didn't have long to wait.

FBI agents arrived at the jail and met with McVeigh. They told him they suspected he may have information about the Oklahoma City bombing and then read the prisoner his rights. McVeigh immediately demanded a lawyer.

The commotion of the FBI's arrival in helicopters had attracted the local populace in Perry. With the media hot on the trail of the investigation as well, it was rumored that someone inside the jail had been involved in the bombing. When McVeigh was informed he would be moved to a more secure facility for questioning, his face registered fear.

"I want a bulletproof vest," he demanded.

"No," he was told.

"I don't want to die like Jack Ruby," McVeigh insisted.

The answer was still no.

"Then take me off the roof by chopper."

Again, McVeigh was told no. The roof was not suitable for a helicopter.

Outside the jail, McVeigh could hear a crowd gathering and the situation was getting worrisome. "Bring him out," they shouted. "Murderer!" "Baby Killer!"

McVeigh steeled himself, as the agents led him from the police station to a waiting car, amid screams of "Kill the creep!"

About the same time, a similar scene was playing out in Herington, Kansas. About 200 miles (322 km) away from Perry, a 40-year-old man named Terry Nichols arrived at the local police station. Word quickly spread among locals that someone involved in the bombing was inside, and the same angry response was brewing on the street.

For days, the media had been fueling rumors it had likely been foreign nationals who committed the bombing attack. Suddenly, it appeared that the threat had come from within U.S. borders, from men who considered themselves patriots. The reality that an American would do such a thing seemed too incredible to believe, and the public devoured any bit of information the media could divulge.

Scenes of McVeigh's arrest were constantly replayed on national television, as broadcasters explained what they knew about this mysterious homegrown terrorist.

McVeigh, it appeared, had been born April 23, 1968. He was one of three children raised in Pendleton, New York. Broadcasters described his childhood as normal. Timothy was described as a typical kid next door. The images of an average clean-cut American boy like "Timmy" were juxtaposed against the devastation in Oklahoma City, and the images stunned the nation.

Pendleton was a small town near the Canadian border that had been established by a rugged individualist named Sylvester Pendleton Clark. Clark had led a rebellion against the government to protest taxation in the early 1880s. Pendleton was a proud community that was shocked to learn one of their own had followed in Clark's footsteps more than a century later.

McVeigh had been a well-liked boy. His father, Bill, was employed in a blue-collar job there. His deceased grandfather, Eddie, had been an avid outdoorsman like so many other men in the area, and had been respected in the community. They all asked themselves how such a thing could come of one of their own.

But the road to the Murrah Building had taken many twists since the days when little "Timmy" had shoveled walks in Pendleton. He had started to become a fiercely independent sort as early as age 13. His grandfather had presented the boy with a .22 caliber rifle when he turned 13, and from that moment on, Timothy's life revolved around firearms. While other boys in his school dreamed of becoming pilots and firemen, Timothy wanted to become a gun shop owner. He was proud of the growing collection of firearms he was amassing, even as a teenager. In fact, he often took guns to school to impress his schoolmates.

At home, his affection for firearms was considered normal, but his family life was not average. As he grew up, Timothy witnessed a great deal of anger and resentment between his parents. His father was a quiet, hardworking man, but his mother had a wild streak. She liked to party and stay out late. His parents were like oil and water and finally, after years of fighting, they separated. In 1986—the year Timothy graduated from high school with honors—the couple divorced.

At that time, McVeigh had been working at a local fast food restaurant, but when high school ended, his goals seemed to change. He still wanted to be a gun shop owner, and he spent considerable time researching the Second Amendment and the rights of gun owners in America. Although he complied with his father's wishes to further his education, McVeigh only did a short stint in business college before returning to his job flipping hamburgers, while he looked for a job that involved guns. Eventually, he found one working as an armed guard with an armored car service.

On May 24, 1988, at the age of 20, McVeigh fed his fascination with guns by joining the army; he felt he'd found his calling. The military provided everything he wanted in life. It gave him a sense of discipline that had been lacking in his youth and an opportunity to handle real firepower. In the army, he had an endless supply of weaponry to use, and he loved it. He wanted to hone his skills in the military, perhaps make it a career.

Through basic training in Fort Benning, Georgia, McVeigh was a determined and eager recruit. He had his eyes set on joining the Green Berets. Unfortunately for him, and for the many who died in Oklahoma City years later, McVeigh's life course crossed paths with two other men who had different ambitions.

During his course of training, McVeigh became friends with Terry Lynn Nichols and Michael Fortier.

Nichols had joined the army relatively late in life and was 12 years older than McVeigh in boot camp. He was considered "the old man," and McVeigh built a strong bond with the opinionated fellow recruit. Nichols didn't fit the

FIRST INFANTRY DIVISION

The "Big Red One" (named for the red patch the soldiers wear on their shoulder) is the oldest continuously serving division in the U.S. Army. The Division's history begins in 1917 with the First American Expeditionary Force.

The First Infantry Division deployed 12,000 soldiers and 7,000 pieces of equipment to Saudi Arabia in 1990 in support of Operation Desert Storm, and later led the charge into Iraq.

same mold as McVeigh, however. He was already married and had a son. The strict army regimen McVeigh enjoyed was something Nichols rebelled against. He told his younger friend he'd joined the army only because he couldn't find another job. Later, when Nichols's wife left their marriage, he eagerly took a hardship discharge so he could return home to raise his son.

Fortier, Timothy's other army buddy, was about the same age, but he was also very different from McVeigh. Fortier had likely joined the army because his family had a strong military background, but his attitudes were much more liberal. He reportedly took drugs and smoked pot.

When the trio moved from basic training to their first posting in Fort Riley, Kansas, McVeigh was still enamored of the military. He was an excellent marksman and showed above-average skill with every weapon he was given to use. That made him a valuable military asset in 1991 when the Gulf War erupted.

McVeigh's First Infantry Division was sent to the Persian Gulf as part of the forces participating in Desert Storm. In combat, McVeigh served with distinction. He became a lead gunner on a Bradley Fighting Vehicle because of his marksmanship and skill, and when he returned home after his stint in the Persian Gulf, he had a fist full of medals, including a Bronze Star.

Back on U.S. soil, McVeigh once again pursued his dream of joining the Special Forces. But the training regimen for the Green Berets was simply too difficult for the man who had served with distinction on the field of battle. He no longer had the stamina that was needed and, in spite of his desire and war record, he was cut from the field of candidates during training.

The failure destroyed McVeigh's satisfaction with military life. He suddenly saw it as a drain on his energy rather than as a nurturing career, and he quit and once again returned to being a security guard in the Buffalo, New York area.

Since his high school years, McVeigh had been avidly reading *The Turner Diaries* and when he left the military under a cloud of dissatisfaction, the rebellious plot of the book took on new meaning for him. He could identify with the main character's loathing for government and he began to regularly criticize the administration to his co-workers. He felt let down by the government he'd tried to defend. He saw gun control as an abuse of power, and conspiracy theories lurked in the most harmless news events.

Early in 1993, McVeigh felt a need to reconnect with his army buddies. He quit his job, sold everything he owned, and decided to hit the highway to find the meaning that was missing from his life. He wanted to visit Michael Fortier in Kingman, Arizona, as well as Terry Nichols, who by then was living on his brother's farm in Michigan. Both Fortier and Nichols felt a kinship for McVeigh's anti-government rhetoric, and McVeigh knew he'd be comfortable with either of them.

On his run west, however, something happened to detour McVeigh. On February 28, 1993, federal agents of the Bureau of Alcohol, Tobacco, and Firearms raided a compound in Waco, Texas, run by a group called the Branch Davidians.

McVeigh suspected that the rights of David Koresh and his followers had been violated, and he rushed to witness events as they unfolded. He stocked up on anti-government literature and bumper stickers he could sell to other curious onlookers. When federal agents blocked his attempts to see the compound, McVeigh met a student reporter named Michelle Rauch who was willing to listen to his rants.

In an interview with Rauch, McVeigh gave the first official hints at what would occur in

Oklahoma City. He said: "The government is afraid of the guns people have because they have to have control of the people at all times. Once you take away the guns, you can do anything to the people."

"The government," McVeigh continued, "is continually growing bigger and more powerful, and the people need to prepare to defend themselves against government control."

But Waco was little more than a media circus in McVeigh's opinion, so a few days after arriving, he left Waco bound for Kingman. Once he'd reached Michael Fortier's mobile home, McVeigh relaxed. For a time, the two men enjoyed long talks about politics and the need for action by "patriots," but Fortier's penchant for drugs soon had McVeigh bored. With renewed energy, he decided to continue his trip on to Tulsa to visit a gun show.

McVeigh took in many such shows during his travels to see Fortier and Nichols, because at them he felt he was in the company of comrades. One man he met at the events, Roger Moore, had attitudes so similar to McVeigh's that the two men hit it off immediately. Moore invited McVeigh to visit his ranch in Arkansas, which he did.

At Moore's spread, McVeigh was astounded to find an isolated ranch stocked with weapons and explosives. It would be a place to which he'd return under far less cordial circumstances.

After spending some time with Moore, McVeigh continued to Decker, Michigan, and the Nichols's farm. The standoff in Waco was now national news and with the Nichols brothers beside him, McVeigh soaked up the television coverage. All three agreed that something had to be done to bring the United States back to freedom. Someone had to take a stand. When, on April 19, 1993, the compound was burned, the Nichols told McVeigh that the government's attack on the Branch Davidians was pointless overkill. "Anyone could make explosives," they told McVeigh, "and out of readily available materials." McVeigh listened and was interested, but didn't act on what he was told for some time.

In the year that followed, however, McVeigh felt the crushing grip of government even more. New laws in place by September 1994 had stopped the manufacture of many types of firearms, including some semi-automatic rifles and handguns. By then, McVeigh had started his gun shop business, although he had no storefront, and the new laws had started to cramp his business. He bought guns under his own name, then sold the weapons to others for a brokerage fee. Usually his customers were happy to avoid having their names appear on the registration forms.

From the Nichols home in Marion, Kansas, McVeigh decided to write to Fortier. The time had come for some sort of protest and he was soliciting Michael's help, along with Terry, in acting out a scene from *The Turner Diaries*. As a protest against the federal government's increasing power, he wanted to blow up a federal building somewhere.

Fortier, however, rejected McVeigh's offer. Complaining about the government was one thing; blowing up federal property was an entirely different matter. Fortier responded by telling McVeigh he would not be a party to such action "unless there was a U.N. tank in my front yard"...referring to a theory of McVeigh's that0 a New World Order had made the U.N. its army.

While Fortier's lack of support might have disturbed McVeigh, it didn't deter him or Nichols. The two men began to follow instructions they found in bomb-building manuals, acquiring the ingredients listed in a recipe for explosives. What the two men couldn't buy under an assumed name, they stole—elements such as blasting caps and liquid nitro-methane.

In order to pay for their purchases, McVeigh had an easy solution. Roger Moore's ranch had very little security, considering the valuable collection of firearms, gold, silver, and jewels he kept there. McVeigh decided he would just help himself. Not only did he steal a variety of guns and valuables from Moore at gunpoint, he also took the rancher's van to transport the stolen loot.

Although Fortier wouldn't join McVeigh's plan, he allowed Timothy and Nichols to visit for a period of time and store their stolen explosives in a shed they rented nearby. During the visit, McVeigh demonstrated his bomb-making skills using soup cans. To have a weapon the size he needed, however, would take big drums.

McVeigh wanted to use anhydrous hydrazine to fuel his explosive, but couldn't afford it. He settled for nitro-methane as an alternative. McVeigh called around the country from Fortier's home, looking for supplies. He had purchased a telephone calling card under an alias, but knew full well that a trace by federal authorities would lead to Fortier, and that would be a secret joke on the man who refused to join his tiny terrorist cell.

As preparations for their attack proceeded, McVeigh learned of his grandfather's death in Pendleton, New York. In mid-October 1994, he returned home to settle the estate. During his visit, McVeigh ranted on about the Waco disaster and used a computer owned by his sister, Jennifer, to compose anti-government letters. While in Pendleton, McVeigh was not able to stay in contact with Terry Nichols.

Nichols had decided to use the time to visit his current wife and daughter in the Philippines. Before he departed, however, he left a package with his first wife, with instructions for it not to be opened unless he never returned. His first wife ignored the instructions. Inside the package she found a sealed envelope containing a letter to McVeigh, $20,000, and the combination to a rented storage locker. Curiously addressed to his first wife, the letter told McVeigh he was on his own. Without hesitation, she found the storage locker and opened it. Inside she discovered some of the loot taken from the Moore ranch.

By the middle of December 1994, McVeigh's plan was almost complete. He met with Fortier at his motel in Kingman and had Fortier's wife wrap gift boxes containing blasting caps. McVeigh promised Fortier weapons in return for traveling with him back to Kansas. On the way there, McVeigh showed Fortier the building in Oklahoma City he planned to destroy and the route he planned to take when he walked away. He also explained how he planned to use his 1977 yellow Marquis as his getaway vehicle.

The plan was to have Nichols follow the Marquis in his truck. Once McVeigh had found a safe place to park it away from the bombsite, he removed the license plate, and Nichols drove him to his motel. The following day, McVeigh rented the Ryder truck and parked it at the motel for the night.

Nichols met McVeigh again at the Herington storage unit the next day and loaded the ingredients for the bomb into the truck. At a deserted pullout near Geary Lake, the two men mixed the ingredients for their explosive. Nichols headed back home and McVeigh waited with his device in a vacant lot until dawn.

At sunrise, McVeigh dressed for his mission in his favorite T-shirt. On the front was a picture of Abraham Lincoln and the motto "*sic simper tyrannis*" (thus ever to tyrants). Prophetically, on the back of the shirt were a blood-drenched tree and the words "The tree of liberty must be refreshed from time to time with the blood of patriots and tyrants."

Once McVeigh had completed his mission of death and destruction and had been captured, the American nation watched one of the more expensive trials ever staged in the United States. It opened with media fanfare on April 24, 1997. McVeigh was loathed by the nation. The defense attorneys tried in vain to soften the image of a cold-blooded murderer.

To ensure that both McVeigh and Nichols were treated fairly, Judge Robert Matsch, chief district judge for the District of Colorado, decided the two men would be tried separately.

In the long trial that ensued, McVeigh's attorneys attempted to prove that their client was actually a student of history and a strong supporter of the founding fathers. His arrest was, the attorneys claimed, a case of mistaken identity. But the testimony of McVeigh's sister, Jennifer, and his friend Michael Fortier was damning. Michael's wife, Lori, testified as to how McVeigh had demonstrated his plan for building the truck bomb. She admitted to helping McVeigh by laminating a fake driver's license he could use to rent the Ryder truck.

"We turned the news on early that morning and we seen what happened," Lori told the court. "We saw that the building had been blown up, and I knew right away that it was Tim." She admitted that she knew what his target would be and that she could have acted to stop him by reporting the plan to the police.

McVeigh's legal counsel tried to destroy Lori's credibility, painting her testimony as a badly disguised attempt to exact a lighter sentence for her husband. But the facts were too strong to ignore. McVeigh's sister, Jennifer, appeared as a government witness as well, with the understanding that none of her testimony could be used against her in the future. Her testimony was also damning. Michael Fortier's testimony put the last nails into McVeigh's coffin.

Hard evidence, such as the phone cards he used (which helped authorities track his location), fingerprints on receipts for bomb ingredients, chemical residues on his clothing, and the earplugs he used to shield the noise of the explosion, all pointed to McVeigh's guilt. The jury took three days to decide his fate, however.

Two months later, McVeigh was sentenced to death on each of 11 counts.

While waiting for the execution to be carried out, McVeigh was held in maximum security in Terre Haute, Indiana. Also in this facility were other equally despised terrorists, including Ramzi Yousef, the mastermind behind the World Trade Center bombing on February 26, 1993, and Ted Kaczynski, the notorious Unabomber, serving four life sentences for mail bombings.

Eventually, Terry Nichols also became a guest in the same facility, sentenced for life for his part in the bombing. Reportedly, Nichols refused to speak with McVeigh in prison. Fortier joined them later with a 12-year sentence for failing to alert police to the plot.

McVeigh had been preparing to die since the previous December, when he asked Judge Matsch to waive all future appeals of his death sentence. Matsch complied, but McVeigh's scheduled execution was thrown in to doubt when it was revealed that the FBI had failed to provide more than 4,400 pages of documents to the terrorist's defense. His death sentence was delayed for several weeks, and his attorneys tried in vain to postpone it further.

Timothy McVeigh was put to death by lethal injection at 7:14 a.m. on Monday, June 11, 2001. He had admitted setting the bomb that killed 168 people in the Oklahoma City federal building and had called off further legal efforts to delay the execution. The first federal prisoner to be executed in 38 years, he died minutes after a deadly injection was administered through a needle in his right leg.

Reportedly, McVeigh looked once to the gallery of witnesses, and then wordlessly stared up at the ceiling. He died with his eyes open, probably wishing to the end that his death would be delivered by a bullet instead.

AHMED RESSAM

BORN: MAY 17, 1967

PLACE OF BIRTH: ALGERIA

ALIAS: BENNI ANTOINE NORRIS

CURRENT WHEREABOUTS: IN JAIL

CHAPTER 6

Ahmed Ressam

A hmed Ressam almost entered American history as a mass murderer. He would have preferred to be recorded as a martyr for Islam. All he gained was infamy.

The glory of killing Americans while the world celebrated the new millennium was all the 32-year-old Algerian national thought about for almost a year. He'd scouted the death site, recruited zealot accomplices, and meticulously prepared his murder weapons. As the deadline to mayhem approached, Ressam thought he'd devised a foolproof plan, but he hadn't realized one simple thing: Costco membership cards aren't considered picture ID by U.S. Customs officers on the border between Canada and the United States.

Like an unknown number of his extremist brethren, Ressam had been among a massive population of illegal residents living among North Americans. Three years earlier, the U.S. Immigration and Naturalization Service (INS) had estimated there were 5 million illegal residents hiding in the United States. Between 1981 and 1991, Canada had admitted 279,000 people as permanent residents on humanitarian grounds and, by the time Ressam was living there, Canada had more than 100,000 deportation orders on the books, with a backlog that was growing by 10 per cent a year.

No immigration official in either country knew how many legal or illegal immigrants, or foreign visitors for that matter, were in their respective countries to attempt acts of terror.

Ressam had apparently not moved to Canada with terrorism in mind. He was born in Algeria in 1967, just five years after the French lowered the last tricolor and pulled out of their African colony. When the Islamic Front for Salvation (IFS) gained control of Algeria in the early 1990s, Ressam decided to flee. He'd grown up in a household familiar with western culture and had happily embraced it. The IFS represented the opposite of U.S. cultural ideals. They professed leadership according to the sharia, laws derived from strict interpretations of the Koran. Ressam had a penchant for western designer clothes and a lifestyle filled with nightclubbing and alcohol. Under the IFS, either habit branded him a criminal.

So, on September 5, 1992, he fled the country for Marseilles, France, traveling on a 30-day visitor's visa. Although he was an illegal immigrant, he managed to procure a false French

passport and an airline ticket to Montreal. After arriving in Montreal, he applied for political asylum, and an immigration hearing was
set to review his case the following March. In
the meantime, Ressam was granted monthly
welfare subsistence of $550. When he failed to
appear for his hearing, he was arrested, finger-
printed, and then courteously given a second
chance to appear on another court date.

To supplement his welfare payments, Ressam had been stealing purses and tourist suitcases, as well as shoplifting. He wanted to stay
in Canada, but didn't know how to navigate the
Canadian immigration system. Logically, he
turned to the Algerian immigrants who'd arrived
before him, and the Masjid as-Salam mosque
in Montreal was a perfect place to meet them.
Fateh Kamel, an Algerian who had married a
Canadian, was one of his advisors.

Several years before, French intelligence
officers had uncovered Kamel's name in the
records of an Islamic terrorist with suspected

links to al-Qaeda. The 35-year-old had fought as a mujahedin in Afghanistan and Bosnia and was busy manufacturing false documents for Islamic terrorists. Ressam's skill as a thief interested Kamel. He offered to pay Ressam for whatever passports or identity papers he found in his stolen purses and suitcases. Ressam welcomed the job opportunity and apparently managed to deliver documents at least 40 times, until he was caught as a pickpocket in October 1996.

Despite being convicted for thievery and being an illegal immigrant long past the date of his ordered deportation, Ressam was only fined, and the sentencing judge put him on probation for two years and then released him.

The failure of immigration authorities to act is not an isolated case. A similar series of bureaucratic faux pas occurred with the INS in the United States in the case of a Lebanese Shiite Muslim named Mohammad Youssef Hammoud. Hammoud first entered the United States at 18 years of age on June 6, 1992, with a badly faked U.S. visa. He was caught immediately but allowed to enter the country pending an investigation of his status. Five months later, he requested political asylum, and it took another 13 months for a judge to turn down that request. Hammoud appealed the deportation order and a year later, in December 1994, married a U.S. citizen. It took another 18 months before the INS determined that the marriage was a fake. Again, he was ordered deported, on this occasion in a month's time. But instead of leaving, he stayed, and the INS did little to enforce the order. In May 1997, Hammoud claimed to have married again and, in September, for a third time. Horrendous record keeping failed to track him. Incredibly, he was granted a green card in July 1998 (the INS did not even check if Hammoud had divorced his second wife before marrying the third, which he did not do). In 2003, after the joint task force swoop, he was tried, convicted, and sentenced to 155 years in prison for aiding the terrorist group Hezbollah.

Ressam's work for Kamel gave him some notoriety among Algerian ex-pats, and he was introduced to Abderraouf Hannachi. Hannachi, in his mid-40s, was a regular at the Assuna Annabawiyah mosque where he often held court, openly criticizing what he saw as the West's decadent culture. He called western dress immoral, its music godless. From the safety of the mosque, he worked tirelessly to attract young Muslims like Ressam, encouraging them to join the holy war against the United States.

Hannachi told the young men that he had been trained at one of Osama bin Laden's camps in Afghanistan. At the Khaldun camp, he said, he'd learned how to fire handguns, assault rifles, and grenade launchers. He'd also been taught the secrets of urban warfare, he said, and other young Muslims could do the same. He implored them to heed the call of leaders in the global jihad.

Ressam and his friends were enthralled by the stories Kamel and Hannachi were spinning. At the apartment they shared at 6301 Place de

la Malicorne, they began talking about plans for
their own excursions to participate in the jihad.
What none of them realized was that their con-
versations were being overheard.

The French had alerted the Canadian Security Intelligence Service (CSIS) to Kamel's connections with Islamic terrorists. Putting Kamel
under surveillance led them to Ressam and his
friends, a group the French were calling a terrorist "cell." CSIS, however, saw no real danger
in the idle boasting about jihad they overheard
at the Malicorne apartment. Calling Ressam
and his friends a terrorist cell was hyperbole. In
fact, the CSIS operatives assigned to listening
called the apartment "BOG"—short for "Bunch
of Guys"—and classed the meetings as little
more than terrorist Tupperware parties. Over
time, they compiled a 400-page dossier, but
didn't share the information with the French or
anyone else. CSIS had a job to protect national
security, and there was nothing the group said
that threatened it. But CSIS didn't know Hanna-

chi was a successful recruiter for al-Qaeda and worked closely with Abu Zubaydah, the man who coordinated the entry of all the terrorist group's recruits to Afghanistan.

Hannachi told Abu Zubaydah he had a good recruit with a clean, new identity. To avoid immigration, Ressam had stolen a blank baptismal certificate from a Catholic church. He chose a new birthday and a new name—Benni Antoine Norris—then obtained a legitimate Canadian passport.

On March 16, 1998, Ressam began a journey to Afghanistan and in Peshawar, Pakistan, was met by Abu Zubaydah. Abu Zubaydah outfitted Ressam and sent him, along with a group of other raw recruits, over the Khyber Pass into Afghanistan to Osama bin Laden's Khaldun camp. The Khaldun camp was a small area of four tents and four stone buildings at which as many as 100 recruits at a time, grouped by nationality, received their initial terrorist training. By September, Ressam had graduated and moved on to another camp, Doha, where he was taught bomb-making skills.

In mid-January 1999, the petty thief was transformed into a terrorist willing to sacrifice himself for jihad. His first assignment was to return to North America, buy passports and weapons, and build a bomb that could be used in the United States to destroy a target of his choice at the dawn of the new millennium. Passing through Los Angeles, Ressam decided one of the world's busiest airports would be his target.

Once he returned to Montreal, Ressam went to work. He found two young men who had not been trained by al-Qaeda but wanted to join the jihad, and he was introduced to another from New York. One Montrealer was an old friend, Abdelmajid Dahoumane; a credit-card thief named Mokhtar Haouari was the second. The New Yorker was a con man named Abdelghani Meskini, who never actually met Ressam in person. It was agreed that Haouari would provide money for the operation, Dahoumane would help Ressam make his bomb, and Meskini would help him deliver it to the target.

Ressam was able to buy all the electronics he needed for the bomb off the shelf at electronics stores, and on November 17, 1999, he and Dahoumane flew to Vancouver to build it.

The two men brewed an explosive cocktail—HMTD—made from hexamine, citric acid, and hydrogen peroxide. HMTD is a most unstable explosive concoction, but easy to manufacture.

Using HMTD, Ressam planned to make a military-grade explosive called C4 plastique. After the explosives were made, Dahoumane returned to Montreal, and Ressam began the first leg of his bombing mission, from Vancouver to Seattle. On December 14, 1999, Ressam drove a rented car onto the Port Angeles ferry from Victoria, British Columbia. Arriving in Port Angeles at suppertime that evening, his was the last car to roll off the ferry.

Fortunately for travelers at the Los Angeles

airport, U.S. Customs Inspector Diana Dean would be just as vigilant with the last car she inspected at the Port Angeles ferry dock as she was with her first. She noticed the driver appeared visibly feverish. His one-word answers to her routine questions were clipped and poorly pronounced. To her honed instincts, the man was "hinky."

Dean ordered the man to complete a customs declaration. When he was done, she asked him to get out of his car so she could inspect his trunk. Ressam did so reluctantly.

By that time other customs officers had finished with their own traffic lanes, so they moved over to help Dean process the last vehicle of the day. Dean told them she had a hunch this might be a "load vehicle," which was inspectors' code for a car or truck used to smuggle drugs. Inspector Mark Johnson stepped forward and addressed the driver in Spanish. Ressam replied in French and offered identification—his Costco membership card.

Because this was such a peculiar thing to do, Johnson was now also wary. He asked Ressam to empty his pockets, while other inspectors checked the man's suitcase and the trunk of his car. It took only a few seconds for Inspector Danny Clem to call them to the rear of Ressam's vehicle. Inside the trunk's spare-tire compartment, Clem had uncovered several green bags filled with a white powder, four black boxes, two pill bottles, and two jars of a brown liquid. The inspectors thought they had stumbled on a drug smuggler.

"Based on this discovery," Dean later reported, "an immediate pat down of Ressam was conducted, during which Ressam managed to slip out of his jacket and flee on foot."

Johnson and another Inspector, Mike Chapman, ran after him. Five blocks away, they spotted Ressam crouching on the ground behind a parked car and attempted a capture, but Ressam again bolted. In an intersection, he tried to commandeer a passing car but was unsuccessful, and the inspectors managed their arrest. Once he was subdued, Ressam was put into the custody of Port Angeles police and detained in a patrol car at the terminal. Customs inspectors soon learned they had not found a drug smuggler at all. Instead, Dean had tripped over four timing devices, 118 pounds (53.5 kg) of urea crystals, 14 pounds (6.4 kg) of RDX and HMDT in white powder form, and 48 ounces (1.4 L) of EDGN—a gooey brown liquid like nitroglycerine.

Ressam didn't stand trial until March 13, 2001. After a three-week hearing, a jury found him guilty of nine criminal counts, which included conspiracy to commit an act of international terrorism. Under questioning, Ressam revealed terrifying facts about a group that the general public was only beginning to recognize—al-Qaeda.

CHAPTER 7

Rogues' Gallery

Jamal Ahmed al-Fadl

Jamal Ahmed al-Fadl was known as "Confidential Source One"—CS-1—in the CIA. The information he provided in February 2001 was confirmed by information left on computer disks found in Nairobi, Kenya, after the suicide bombings of U.S. embassies in Kenya and Tanzania that killed 301 people in August 1998.

With the financial support of the Farouq

Mosque in New York, in 1988, al-Fadl left Brooklyn for Peshawar and in the dusty Pakistani border town joined thousands of al-Qaeda recruits fighting a holy war against the Soviets in Afghanistan.

Al-Fadl found his way into an al-Qaeda training camp where he learned to fire a Russian-made Kalashnikov rifle and United States-supplied Stinger surface-to-air rockets. He also learned how to build bombs. After several weeks in training, al-Fadl found himself in the presence of an ascetic Saudi named Osama bin Laden, the new emir (chief) of a group called al-Qaeda. Al-Fadl traveled with bin Laden to the battle-scarred town of Khost, where bin Laden had organized an explosives training camp.

Al-Fadl was psychologically overpowered by the tall Saudi's dream of an Islamic world-state formed through battle and not words. He agreed to join al-Qaeda as one of its founding members, signing an agreement that committed him to the devotion of his life to Allah. He also took the *bayat* (oath of allegiance) to Osama bin Laden. The *bayat* involved a period of fasting, self-castigation with a whip made of small chains, and days of intense indoctrination.

During his period of service, at the end of 1993, Al-Fadl claimed to have been involved in trying to broker a $1.5 million purchase of weapons-grade uranium for bin Laden. The supplier was a former Sudanese government minister who said he represented businessmen from South Africa. Mogadem Salah Abd Al-Mobruk, who had been a lieutenant colonel in the Sudanese Army, had also served as Sudan's minister of justice during the Numeiri presidency (1969–1983).

While he could not verify if a purchase was ever completed, al-Fadl later claimed the uranium had been tested at a facility in Hilat Koko in Cyprus and then transported to Afghanistan.

His adoration for bin Laden didn't last long. Al-Fadl's efforts earned him $10,000 for brokering the uranium deal, but he complained about the compensation he was receiving. Al-Fadl was drawing only a third of what his Egyptian counterparts were receiving, and had been flatly told it was because he was worthless. Angered, al-Fadl decided to steal from the terror master at his first opportunity. After completing a $100,000 theft, he knew his life was in danger, so al-Fadl approached the CIA for protection and became their prime source.

Mohamed Rashed Daoud Al-'Owhali

Mohamed Rashed Daoud Al-'Owhali was barely out of his teens when he moved to Saudi Arabia from Liverpool, England. He was an intense young man who wanted to return to his wealthy parents' homeland, a place he could remember from childhood. Al-'Owhali was a sponge for the teaching of Islam once he arrived in Riyadh to attend a religious university.

Like so many other Arab youth, he was driven by the fervor of jihad-touting clerics, and he joined in the rush to Afghanistan at the age of 21. His first training experience came in the Zahwar Kal al-Badr camp, followed by other al-Qaeda camps in the Hindu Kush Mountains. In them, he was initiated into the absolute secrecy of a holy fraternity of suicide bombers. Eventually, after fighting alongside the fundamentalist Islamic Taliban militia that overthrew the Ahmad Sha Massood government in 1996, al-'Owhali received the most intensive training being provided by al-Qaeda.

In preparation for special operations, he was taught killing techniques with what an al-Qaeda training manual specified were "cold steel weapons (wire, knife, rod); poisons, pistols, rifles; and, explosives." He was also instructed in methods of physical and psychological torture and was finally assigned to the Third Martyr's Barracks, First Squad, of the El Bara Bin Malik Division of the Army of Liberating the Islamic Holy Lands.

Al-'Owhali didn't have to wait long for his first assignment. He was ordered to shave his beard and report to another terrorist cell in Yemen. Once there, his commanders supplied him with a new name and passport. He became Abdul Ali Latif and was put back into training. In Yemen he received instruction in security while on a mission and then, two years later, another name and another passport.

Now a Yemeni named Khalid Salim Saleh bin Rashid, al-'Owhali returned to Pakistan for his first assignment. In Pakistan, al-'Owhali was told he was headed for martyrdom. His task was to help detonate a truck laden with explosives within the grounds of an enemy embassy in East Africa. After that, his al-Qaeda commander assured him, he would enter paradise and receive his reward of 72 *houris* (virgins).

Al-'Owhali was ecstatic about his good fortune to have been given such an important assignment, and he traveled to Nairobi dreaming of the paradise he would soon be entering. His job was not to drive the truck, but to use stun grenades on the embassy guards, lift the gate to allow the truck to enter the embassy grounds, and then join the driver in martyrdom. Al-'Owhali did what was required. Unfortunately for him, while the driver was killed by the blast, he only received cuts and bruises and was quickly captured by the U.S. military.

Serving a life sentence in the United States, he now accepts with bitterness the fact that his dream of paradise in return for martyrdom will always be just that—a dream.

Mahmud Abouhalima

He was known amongst his fellow terrorists as "Mahmud the Red." Born in 1959 in Kafr al-Dawar, Egypt, he was the first of four sons of a mill foreman.

As a teenager, Abouhalima joined the Egyptian Islamic Group, a fundamentalist extremist group that considers Sheik Omar Abdel-Rahman to be its spiritual guide.

In September 1981, Abouhalima sought political asylum in Munich, Germany, claiming that he faced persecution in his native land because of his membership in the Muslim Brotherhood, but his request was denied a year later. In order to remain in Germany, Abouhalima proposed to a 34-year-old German nurse named Renate Soika, and they were married in December. The marriage lasted until February 1985, and even before the divorce was finalized, he married another German woman named Marianne Weber in a Muslim ceremony.

Ostensibly traveling on a three-week visit, the couple flew to the United States in the fall of 1985, settled in Brooklyn, and never returned to Germany. Just six months later, Abouhalima's tourist visa expired, but it coincided with an amnesty the U.S. Congress had passed for more than one million illegal aliens then residing in the country. Abouhalima applied for amnesty in 1986 and received temporary legal residency in 1988, becoming a permanent resident two years after that.

Abouhalima got a chauffeur's license and worked as a taxi driver in New York for the next five years. He was a poor driver and had his license suspended 10 times for failing to appear in court for traffic violations. During any available time, Abouhalima volunteered with a Brooklyn non-profit group raising money for the Afghan mujehadin. Once he received his green card, Abouhalima took several trips to Peshawar, Pakistan, and between 1988 and 1990 received combat training in al-Qaeda camps.

In 1990, when Sheik Omar moved to the United States, Abouhalima became the Islamic Group leader's part-time bodyguard and driver.

On March 5, 1993, a week after a bomb attack on the World Trade Center, Abouhalima fled the United States. He made his way from Jeddah, Saudi Arabia, to his hometown in Egypt, where he was captured by authorities. Under interrogation, he confessed to participation in the bombing and was extradited to the United States to stand trial.

A year later, he and three co-defendants were convicted of conspiracy, explosives charges, and assault for the World Trade Center bombing. He received a sentence of 240 years in prison with no possibility of parole.

Saif Al-Adel

Wanted in connection with the August 7, 1998 bombing of U.S. embassies in Dar es Salaam, Tanzania, and Nairobi, Kenya, there is a $5 million bounty offered for Saif Al-Adel's capture and conviction.

Al-Adel is thought to be affiliated with Egyptian Islamic Jihad (EIJ) and is believed to be a high-ranking member of the al-Qaeda organization in Afghanistan. His current whereabouts are unknown.

He is wanted by the FBI on charges of conspiracy to kill U.S. nationals, to destroy buildings and property of the United States, and to destroy the national defense utilities of the United States.

Ibrahim Salih Mohammed Al-Yacoub

Ibrahim Salih Mohammed Al-Yacoub is wanted by the FBI for conspiracy to kill U.S. nationals, conspiracy to murder U.S. employees, conspiracy to use weapons of mass destruction against U.S. nationals, conspiracy to destroy property of the United States, conspiracy to attack national defense utilities, bombing resulting in death, use of weapons of mass destruction against U.S. nationals, murder while using destructive device during a crime of violence, murder of federal employees, and attempted murder of federal employees.

Al-Yacoub was indicted for the June 25, 1996, bombing of the Khobar Towers in Dhahran, Saudi Arabia. His current whereabouts are unknown.

Abdullah Ahmed Abdullah

Abdullah Ahmed Abdullah is considered by U.S. authorities to be one of the most violent terrorists currently at large. Reportedly, he sleeps with an AK-47 on his bedside, rarely rests for more than 4 to 5 hours each night, and never sleeps in the same place.

He is wanted by the FBI on charges of murder of U.S. nationals outside the United States, conspiracy to murder U.S. nationals outside the United States, attack on a federal facility resulting in death, conspiracy to kill U.S. nationals, to destroy buildings and property of the United States, and to destroy the national defense utilities of the United States.

He was indicted for involvement in the August 7, 1998, bombings of the U.S. embassies in Dar es Salaam, Tanzania, and Nairobi, Kenya. His current whereabouts are unknown.

Ted Kaczynski

Until Ted Kaczynski began his nearly 18-year campaign of terror, Americans had rarely experienced the violence gripping other parts of the world.

But the "Unabomber" changed that.

Kaczynski was born in Chicago on May 22,

1942, and had enjoyed a brilliant academic career. He seemed sane enough until a few months after his 36th birthday.

On May 25, 1978, an undelivered parcel was returned to Professor Buckley Crist of Northwestern University in Evanston, Illinois. Crist appeared to be the sender of a carefully wrapped package that was found in the parking lot at the University of Chicago and addressed to E. J. Smith, a professor of engineering at the Rensselaer Polytechnic Institute in Troy, New York.

Because Crist had no knowledge of the package, he gave it to campus security, and unfortunately, Terry Marker, the security guard on duty, became the first in a long sequence of people to be anonymously injured by the Unabomber.

The pipe bomb inside the package was an amateurish contraption: it had been made out of a wooden box with a primitive trigger device that ignited explosive powders. However, it was powerful enough to send Marker to the hospital with hand injuries.

No one knew why Professors Crist or Smith had been targeted. Investigators felt that the attack was likely the work of a disgruntled student. No one had any reason to believe it was a serial bomber's first attack—until a year later.

On May 9, 1979, John G. Harris, a civil engineering graduate student found a cigar box abandoned in room 2424 at Northwestern University. It was fastened with tape and, when opened, disintegrated in a forceful explosion. Though it was noisy, this bomb left Harris with only minor abrasions from wooden debris.

Investigators began to take worried notice. The wooden box style of bomb looked like a signature, and it appeared that the bomber was learning his craft. The primitive trigger used with the first bomb—a nail tensioned with rubber bands—had been replaced with a battery-powered filament that quickly ignited the explosive powders in the box. And the perpetrator had taken great care to remove any identifying markings on the batteries, so tracing their source was impossible.

* * *

American Airlines flight 444 was en-route from Chicago to Washington on a standard milk run until the Boeing 727 reached the altitude of 35,500 feet. When that happened, passengers on the plane were alarmed to hear a loud explosion in the baggage compartment.

A parcel containing gunpowder and a common household barometer rigged to function as an altimeter, had exploded and was smoldering. Noxious smoke filled the cabin, forcing the deployment of oxygen masks and an emergency landing at Dulles International Airport. Passengers were evacuated onto the tarmac using the plane's escape slide, and 12 were rushed to hospital to be treated for smoke inhalation. On examination, investigators found another crude bomb made in a wooden box—and realized they had a repeater to contend with. This time, the bomb had been mailed, so besides Alcohol, Tobacco, and Firearms personnel, the investigation included agents from the U.S. Postal Service and the FBI.

New odd twists developed in the bomber's style, too. Besides the trademark wooden box, the bomb had been equipped with barium nitrate, a chemical used in fireworks that produced green smoke. Investigators wondered if the color was important.

Things became even more puzzling in early June 1980. That month, United Airlines president, Percy Wood, received a letter and a book allegedly sent by Enoch Fischer of Lake Forest, Illinois. When Wood opened the book, an explosive device inside its hollowed pages exploded in his hands. While the victim sustained considerable injuries, none were life threatening. However, the combination of trademarks that came with the incident had investigators pondering.

The parcel had been addressed in green ink. The term "wood" was obviously used over and over. The package had been sent to Percy Wood; wood was included inside to serve as shrapnel; the logo for the book's publisher was a leaf; and the false return address was Ravenswood Street. Metal pieces in the bomb were purposefully stamped with the initials FC, which was another mystery.

Following the attack on Percy Wood, the FBI identified the case as UnAbom, an acronym for his targets—UNiversities and Airlines BOMbings.

It was 16 months before another bomb appeared with the "FC" signature. On October 8, 1981, it was discovered at the University of Utah, but disarmed. There didn't seem to be any rhyme or reason to the schedule. It took another seven months before the Unabomber reappeared. This time, the bomb was mailed to a professor at Brigham Young University in Provo, Utah. A secretary who opened the package was severely hurt. Then, a long series of bombing events began:

On July 2, 1982, Professor Diogenes J. Angelakos in Berkeley, California, was badly injured by a bomb that used gasoline as a propellant for metal shrapnel stored inside.

Three years later, a Berkeley grad student with dreams of becoming an astronaut lost four fingers and partial sight in one eye because of another bomb. This one used a mix of ammonium nitrate and aluminum powder and again, remnants found showed the bomb had been stamped "FC."

The following month, on June 13, 1985, the attack was centered on Boeing in Auburn, Washington, but it was aborted by an alert mail clerk.

On June 15, 1985, a book bomb was mailed to a University of Michigan psychology professor. It exploded and injured a secretary and the professor.

A bomb disguised as scrap wood exploded in a parking lot behind the Rentech Computer Store in Sacramento, California, December 11, 1985, killing the storeowner.

On February 20, 1987, a bomb resulted in severe injury to the vice-president of CAAMS, Inc., a Salt Lake City computer firm. Witnesses noticed a stranger outside of the computer store. Their observations resulted in the first visual identification of the suspect and a sketch of a man in a hooded sweatshirt wearing aviator sunglasses was widely circulated.

Then, six years passed before the Unabomber struck again, with a fury.

On June 18, 1993, geneticist Dr. Charles Epstein of the University of California, San Francisco, received a package. On opening it, he lost three fingers.

Dr. David Gelernter, an associate computer science professor at Yale University received a package about the same time. On opening it, he lost part of one hand. (After these two injuries, a statement was mailed to *The New York Times*, claiming credit for the bombings by the "FC.")

On December 10, 1994, advertising executive Thomas Mosser was killed by a letter bomb.

On April 24, 1995, California Forestry Association President Gilbert Murray was killed by a letter bomb.

The letter bombs were followed by regular mail that confirmed the Unabomber's perceived enemies: the computer industry, progress, genetic engineering, and destroyers of the environment. The so-called Unabomber also demanded his "Manifesto" be published. It was the lucky break that solved all the mysteries when David Kaczynski recognized the writing as that of his brother, Ted.

Six weeks later, on April 13, 1996, the investigating agents on the Unabomber Task Force raided Ted Kaczynski's ramshackle cabin outside Lincoln, Montana, and discovered overwhelming proof that they'd nabbed their killer.

Ted Kaczynski's trial was brief after a number of delays required to determine his mental competence. When it was established, he was allowed to represent himself, and he cut a deal with the prosecution to avoid a death penalty.

Kaczynski pleaded guilty to 13 counts for attacks in three states that killed three people and injured two others. He received four consecutive life sentences without chance of parole and today resides in the Colorado "Supermax" prison.

Ayman al-Zawahiri

For most of his life, Ayman al-Zawahiri, the bespectacled "surgeon of the Hindu Kush," has held an abiding hatred for the United States—the culture he considers the enemy of Islam. In June 2001, his group—Egyptian Islamic Jihad—merged with al-Qaeda and, although Osama bin Laden has been the figurehead of Islamic terrorism since then, al-Zawahiri has been a

ALIASES
Ayman al-Zawahiri is known by many different names:
Abdel Moez
Abdel Muaz
Abdel Muez
Abu Abdallah
Abu al-Mu'iz
Abu Fatima
Abu Mohammed
Abu Mohammed Nur al-Deen
Muhammad Ibrahim
Nur
The Doctor
The Teacher
Ustaz

guiding light for terrorism internationally.

Ayman al-Zawahiri has reportedly been the man responsible for much of the planning of terrorism operations waged against the United States since the merge. He masterminded the strategy for the assault on U.S. soldiers in Somalia in 1993, for the bombings of U.S. embassies in East Africa in 1998, for the floating attack on the USS *Cole* in the Yemen harbor in 2000, and for the devastating aerial attack on the World Trade Center and the Pentagon in 2001. The United States offers a $25 million bounty on Ayman al-Zawahiri's head, and for a brief period, believed he was dead—while DNA testing was being conducted on a skull recovered by a Canadian soldier in Afghanistan. The hope of the U.S. military was short-lived, however. No DNA match was made, so it is assumed Ayman al-Zawahiri continues to live and incite violence from somewhere in Pakistan or Afghanistan.

Unlike Osama bin Laden, whose development as a leader of extremist Islam was comparatively sudden, Ayman al-Zawahiri's life has been a steady continuum of militancy. His family has a long history of involvement in the religious and scientific affairs of Egypt. The name al-Zawahiri is associated with a medical dynasty there. His father, Dr. Rabie al-Zawahiri, was a professor of pharmacology at Ain Shams University in Cairo; his uncle, a dermatologist. Of 46 members of his family mentioned in a 1995 obituary in a Cairo newspaper in 1995, 31 were listed as doctors, chemists, or pharmacists. There was also an ambassador, a judge, and a member of parliament among the prominent family mentioned. His father's uncle, Mohammed al-Ahmadi al-Zawahiri, was the Grand Imam of Al-Azhar—the center of Islamic study in the Middle East in the late 1920s. His mother, Umayma, also has a family history of prominence in the Middle East. Her father was the president of Cairo University and the founder of King Saud University in Riyadh. Her father's uncle was a founder of the Arab League.

Al-Zawahiri, therefore, joined generations of academic and political achievers when he and his twin sister, Umnya, were born on June 19, 1951, in the outskirts of a middle-class suburb of Cairo called Maadi.

Like the rest of his siblings who became doctors or architects, al-Zawahiri was among the brightest in his secondary school and university classes. He grew up in a traditional Islamic home on the edges of a cosmopolitan and secular neighborhood, and seemed throughout his youth to lean more toward tradition than a westernized culture. As a child, he was a bookworm who devoutly attended prayers and avoided sports. According to his uncle, Mahfouz Azzam, al-Zawahiri "used to write poetry to his mother" and was deeply religious. To his classmates, he seemed aloof and introverted, at least until his university years.

About the time al-Zawahiri was born, Egypt was in the throes of an Islamic fundamentalist revolution. The Society of Muslim Brothers, one of the oldest fundamentalist groups in Egypt, had fomented an uprising against the British occupying the Suez. The riots they instigated helped a military junta (dominated by army colonel Gamal Abdel Nasser) to overthrow the government of King Farouk in July 1952. Once in control, Nasser tried to hobble the revolutionary leaders of the Muslim Brothers, but their religious grip on the hearts of the common people of Egypt was too great. Nasser faced an ideological struggle for power that eventually resulted in a crackdown on the Muslim Brothers. Thousands were imprisoned, and the torture and execution of their leadership is said to have spawned an appetite for revenge amongst acolytes, which later included al-Zawahiri. The West was seen as the enabling force behind the repressive Nasser regime, and their all-consuming mission for retribution—what they called "justice"—has never been forgotten.

In 1966, Sayyid Qutb, a writer and critic— the voice of the fundamentalist revolution—

was hanged. His ideas, however, had formed the nucleus of a modern Islamic jihad movement in Egypt by then, and a high school student named al-Zawahiri picked up his torch. The same year that Qutb was hanged, al-Zawahiri helped form an underground network of militants among students at Maadi High School. The cell members were dedicated to the replacement of the secular Egyptian government with an Islamic one.

As boys, the militant cell members met in each other's homes, in a mosque, or along the banks of the Nile in isolated locations. They had no means to conduct their revolution, but the five members maintained their aspirations in secret anyway. They were just one of many such clandestine groups of restless and alien-ated students that were forming across Egypt. When their country went to war with Israel in 1967 and was decisively humiliated in six days, the groups seemed to be galvanized against the secular regime ruling Egypt. As fundamental

Islamists, they wanted to see their country restored to the caliphate—the rule of Islamic clerics—which they saw as the only way to regain their pride and build a future. Al-Zawahiri was among the young men who fervently believed in that solution.

A memoir al-Zawahiri published in serial form in a London-based Arabic newspaper in 2001 recalled that time and those objectives. Once Egypt was restored to the caliphate, he wrote, "... history would make a new turn, God willing, in the opposite direction against the empire of the United States and the world's Jewish government."

When Nasser died of a heart attack in 1970, his successor, Anwar Sadat, looked to the Muslim Brotherhood with fear. He attempted to build a bridge with the revolutionaries by emptying the prisons and allowing them a voice, not realizing just how dangerous a threat they posed to his regime. Though the Muslim Brothers were forbidden from forming a political party, they worked tirelessly at recruiting a new band of fundamentalists in the nation's universities, and a new group called Al-Gama'a al-Islamiyya—the Islamic Group—gained a militant foothold. They acquired weapons and radicalized Egypt's campuses, and by 1974, al-Zawahiri's militant cell had grown to 40 members.

At Cairo University medical school where al-Zawahiri was specializing in surgery, the campus was a cauldron of Islamic extremism. By the late 1970s, the various militant groups had become aware of each other and they coalesced into an even newer organization calling itself the Egyptian Islamic Jihad, under the leadership of a young intellectual named Kamal Habib.

Once al-Zawahiri graduated from medical school in 1974, he spent three years working as a surgeon in the Egyptian Army on a base just outside Cairo. Because of his traditional beliefs, he had not dated during his university years, but by 1978 had found the woman who would become his wife through an arranged introduction. Their domestic life without political activism lasted only a few years. In the summer of 1980, al-Zawahiri later recalled that "a twist of fate" brought him to Afghanistan.

Al-Zawahiri was filling in for another doctor at the Muslim Brothers' clinic in Cairo when the director of the clinic appealed to al-Zawahiri to join him in a mercy mission. He wanted al-Zawahiri to accompany him to Pakistan, where they could tend to Afghan refugees. Al-Zawahiri agreed without hesitation. He had been consumed with the task of establishing a base for his jihad in Egypt, but had been unable to do so. The country's topography made it nearly impossible to create a secret locus where militant fighters might gather and be trained as guerillas. Afghanistan offered him an opportunity, he decided, from which he could export his militancy.

With an anesthesiologist and a plastic surgeon, al-Zawahiri was among the first Arab

medicos to go to Pakistan and participate in
relief work. He served with the Red Crescent
Society—the Islamic arm of the Red Cross—in
Peshawar, Pakistan, for four months. His experience among the 1.4 million Afghan refugees who
had been uprooted by 1980 was life changing.
When he returned to Cairo that fall, he was full
of stories about the "miracles" of courage he'd
witnessed taking place in the jihad against the
Soviets. By March 1981, he was ready to return
for another tour of duty with the Red Crescent
Society, but this time stayed only two months.
In his memoir, al-Zawahiri said he regarded the
Afghan conflict as "a training course of the ut-
most importance to prepare the Muslim mujehadin to wage their awaited battle against the
superpower that now has sold dominance over
the globe, namely, the United States."

Al-Zawahiri still envisioned an Islamic state
in Egypt and was waiting for the moment when
the Islamic Jihad had enough strength to act
and overthrown the secular government. One of

his cell members—Isam al-Qamari—had taken on the leadership role and had been working to build up a stock of weapons. Some were even stored in al-Zawahiri's medical clinic in Maadi.

In February 1981, government forces intercepted a transfer of weapons from the clinic to a warehouse. Police arrested a man carrying guns and military maps, and the incident raised alarms for Anwar Sadat's regime. They suddenly realized a new threat was boiling unseen among the fundamentalist Islamic underground. It took several months, but in September, Sadat acted to quash what he could. An estimated 1,500 people were rounded up and arrested, although the dragnet missed snagging al-Zawahiri and the cell's leader, Qamari. For Sadat, the action was too little too late.

A military cell among the broken ranks of the Islamic Jihad already had a plot in place. A hastily conceived plan by a young army recruit named Khaled Islambouli was destined to take their struggle to a new level. On October 6, 1981,

Sadat was reviewing a parade when Islambouli
and three other conspirators leaped out of the
crowd, threw grenades into the reviewing stand,
and riddled the president's body with bullets. For
unknown reasons, al-Zawahiri did not flee Egypt
immediately. At the end of the month he determined to leave on another journey to Pakistan,
and on the drive to the airport, he was arrested.

Al-Zawahiri, defendant No. 113 among
more than 300 militants accused of being involved in the Sadat assassination, was kept in a
four by eight cell in a 12th century fortress on a
hill above Cairo. Intent on capturing the leader
of al-Zawahiri's cell—Qamari—police regularly
tortured al-Zawahiri for information. They took
over his home and waited for the moment when
Qamari might reveal himself. Eventually he did.
Thanks to the identification offered by al-Zawahiri, Qamari, too, was arrested. In his memoir,
al-Zawahiri almost apologizes for his slip of
character. "The toughest thing about captivity
is forcing the Mujahid, under the force of tor-

ture, to confess about his colleagues, to destroy his movement with his own hands, and offer his and his colleagues' secrets to the enemy."

At his trial, al-Zawahiri testified against his friend and 13 others. But the humiliation was something he never forgot, and it helped vault him into the role of spokesman for the militants. Al-Zawahiri's crime in the case of the assassination of Sadat, was the possession of a gun. At the opening day of the trial on December 4, 1982, as the appointed spokesman for the accused militants, al-Zawahiri shouted scurrilous accusations against the regime that imprisoned him, the United States, and the global Jewish threat he saw to Islam.

Al-Zawahiri spent three years in prison. By the time he was released in 1984, he was a hardened radical but had, on the surface at least, decided to step away from politics. He thought of applying for a fellowship in England, but decided to take a job at a clinic in Jidda instead and finally arrived there in 1985. Al-Zawahiri was then 34 years old. He was pious and embittered.

He decided to return to Peshawar and set up a household that was comprised of a two-story villa to shelter his growing family. By 1987, according to reports by Egyptian intelligence, he had reorganized Islamic Jihad there, recruiting new members from the Egyptian mujahedin.

Al-Zawahiri concentrated his efforts to get close to Osama bin Laden, a man he saw as a heaven-sent blessing to his extremist mission. Eventually, al-Zawahiri managed to place several trusted members of Islamic Jihad into key positions around bin Laden and was receiving the bulk of his financing from the Arab. In the cave hideouts of the Hindu Kush, bin Laden became dependent on al-Zawahiri for medical care. Bin Laden, who may suffer from hypoglycemia, apparently regularly received glucose administered by the doctor. (In the case of a hypoglycemic individual, extremely low blood glucose levels, which can be caused by a combination of poor diet and physical exertion, can result in a coma. The administration of glucose can stabilize blood sugar levels.)

Around 1989, a meeting took place in the Afghan town of Khost. At a mujahedin camp, a group of 10 men gathered to form a new organization that could wage jihad beyond the borders of Afghanistan. That group was to be called al-Qaeda and its leader—the man with the money—was Osama bin Laden. That same year, bin Laden returned to Saudi Arabia and the family business.

In 1990, when Saddam Hussein ordered the Iraqi invasion of Kuwait, bin Laden approached the Saudi royal family and offered to defend the oil fields with mujahedin who had returned from Afghanistan. The royal family opted to accept U.S. troop support instead, apparently promising bin Laden that the U.S. soldiers would be expelled after the Gulf War. Two years later, when the troops remained in Saudi Arabia, bin Laden felt betrayed. He returned to

Afghanistan and began preaching against the Saudi regime and funding the activities of Saudi dissidents.

By 1992, infighting among various factions of mujahedin in Afghanistan convinced bin Laden to escape Kabul for Sudan. He took his three wives and 15 children to Khartoum, where he began to establish a corporate empire that could be used to fund Islamic terrorists. Throughout this time, bin Laden continued to fund al-Zawahiri's clinic in Maadi, but al-Zawahiri felt he was unable to return to Egypt for fear of imprisonment.

Instead, al-Zawahiri joined bin Laden in Sudan under the protection of its leader, Hassan al-Tourabi. Tourabi, a graduate of the University of London and the Sorbonne, was trying to establish an Islamic republic based on *sharia*, something al-Zawahiri had been longing for most of his life. In Khartoum, al-Zawahiri again began to reorganize Islamic Jihad. Unfortunately for al-Zawahiri, the funding he expected from bin Laden was meager and inconsistent. Bin Laden was frustrated by the competition for dominance that existed among the key Egyptian militant organizations and refused to fund any of them. Bin Laden wanted the Egyptian members of Islamic Jihad under his direct control, but al-Zawahiri objected.

Although the United States represented the enemy, that is where al-Zawahiri turned for money in a bid to keep his authority alive. He visited California and toured the mosques there in hopes of generating donations. The money he gathered, however, was insignificant and upon his return to Khartoum al-Zawahiri was forced to put his members directly on the al-Qaeda payroll as bin Laden demanded. To al-Zawahiri, it was a marriage of convenience that allowed his members to continue to concentrate their efforts in Egypt thanks to the Saudi's bank accounts. In fact, al-Zawahiri is claimed to have told one of his key advisors that "joining with bin Laden [was] the only solution to keeping the jihad organization alive."

Islamic Jihad saw Sudan as the ideal staging ground for attacks on Egypt. The border was a long, trackless wasteland without guards, over which weapons and explosives supplied by Iran could easily be moved. Islamic Jihad began its assault in August 1993, with an attempt on the life of the Egyptian interior minister who had been responsible for a crackdown on Islamic extremists. A bombing attempt failed. This was followed in November by a plot to kill the prime minister. A car bomb exploded as the prime minister's car passed near a Cairo girl's school. Twenty-one people were injured and one girl was killed, but the prime minister escaped injury. The little girl's death outraged Egyptians. In an attempt to mollify the family, al-Zawahiri offered her parents blood money.

Innovations in martyrdom

Al-Zawahiri became a pioneer in the use of suicide bombers and instituted what has become a traditional act of taping the bomber's vows before a mission. He developed an ultra-secret structure in the jihad group, which meant individual cells were unaware of each other's operations or personnel. Despite his precautions, in 1993, Egyptian authorities managed to capture Islamic Jihad's membership director and his computer. With that arrest, they gained the complete database for the organization. As a result, Egyptian security arrested 1,000 suspects and put 300 of them on trial for sedition. It effectively crippled Islamic Jihad in Egypt. For Islamic Jihad to survive, al-Zawahiri had to look somewhere outside of that country and come up with a momentous act that could be a new watershed for the group.

In the early 1990s, both Islamic Jihad and the Islamic Group were being decimated by defections and arrests. Al-Zawahiri thought of a solution. At a secret meeting in Khartoum in April 1995, with the remaining members of the two organizations and other terrorist groups attending, he proposed the assassination of Egyptian President Hosni Mubarak. Everyone agreed, although the risk was enormous for al-Zawahiri's movement. An assassination attempt on Mubarak was staged in June in Addis Ababa, Ethopia, but the president escaped injury. In retribution, Mubarak instituted what he hoped would be a final crushing blow to Islamic Jihad. Massive numbers of Islamists were arrested (some reports place the numbers as high as 60,000, necessitating the building of five new prisons). Al-Zawahiri retaliated by having members blow up the Egyptian embassy in Islamabad, Pakistan.

In a tit-for-tat move, the Egyptians created a plan to kill al-Zawahiri with a bomb. The scheme involved entrapment of two sons of Islamic Jihad members and having one of them plant a suitcase of explosives near al-Zawahiri. In the final stages of the plot, however, the boy was spotted by Sudanese intelligence and arrested with the suitcase. Both boys involved were jailed and, at al-Zawahiri's request, released to him for questioning. Al-Zawahiri promised to return the youths unharmed, but instead convened an Islamic court and had them sentenced to death as an example to anyone else considering betrayal.

The Sudanese were enraged by al-Zawahiri's trick and bending to pressure from Saudi Arabia and the United States, decided to expel bin Laden, al-Zawahiri, and all of their followers. In May 1996, bin Laden was forced to flee to Jalalabad in Afghanistan, reportedly losing as much as $300 million in investments in Sudan. Al-Zawahiri apparently fled elsewhere. Some reports claim it was Switzerland and others Holland. From articles that appeared in the Wall Street Journal, it was also claimed he traveled to Chechnya to re-establish the Islamic Jihad there.

In early 1997, al-Zawahiri and two of his aides were arrested attempting to illegally enter the Russian province of Dagestan. The Russians found false identity papers, including a Sudanese passport that indicated he had been to Yemen four times, Malaysia three times, Singapore twice, and China once within the previous year and a half. At his trial in April, al-Zawahiri was sentenced to six months in jail, but as he had already served most of that time awaiting trial, he was released soon after. Because Islamic Jihad had been crushed in Egypt, al-Zawahiri and his family had little alternative but to rejoin bin Laden in Jalalabad.

Making the U.S. a target

Within a year, al-Zawahiri had conducted a study of what he saw as Jewish influence in the United States and decided that it was a justified target for Islamic Jihad. Bin Laden rewarded him for his decision by contributing more to the Islamic Jihad annual budget, raising it from $300,000 to $500,000. It was a formal sign that al-Zawahiri had finally sealed the fate of Islamic Jihad to al-Qaeda, which was confirmed by the fact that al-Zawahiri signed a statement on

February 23, 1998, announcing the formation of the International Islamic Front for Jihad on the Jews and Crusaders.

"In compliance with God's order, we issue the following *fatwa* to all Muslims," the announcement said. "The ruling to kill the Americans and their allies—civilian and military—is an individual duty for every Muslim who can do it in any country in which it is possible to do it."

Al-Zawahiri resigned as the emir of Islamic Jihad in the summer of 1999, angered by criticism of his leadership and what he saw as armchair militants. He called them "the hot-blooded revolutionary strugglers who have now become as cold as ice after they have experienced the life of civilization and luxury, the guarantees of the new world order, the gallant ethics of civilized Europe, and the impartiality and materialism of Western civilization."

In June 2001, Islamic Jihad merged into one entity called Qaeda al-Jihad, but by that time it had reportedly dwindled to only 40 members.

Following the attack on the World Trade Center in September 2001, bin Laden and al-Zawahiri appeared on a videotape.

Zawahiri appeared to be healthy and happy about the news. "This great victory was possible only by the grace of God," he said proudly. "This was not just a human achievement—it was a holy act. These 19 brave men who gave their lives for the cause of God will be well taken care of. God granted them the strength to do what they did. There's no comparison between the power of these 19 men and the power of America, and there's no comparison between the destruction these 19 men caused and the destruction America caused."

A few weeks after the September 11 attacks, Interpol issued an arrest warrant for al-Zawahiri. The warrant alleged he "masterminded several terrorist operations in Egypt" and accused him of "criminal complicity and management for the purpose of committing premeditated murder."

Reports not long after from Pakistani intelligence claimed al-Zawahiri had been killed by mercenaries along with other al-Qaeda fighters. It was alleged they buried his remains in a snow bank. The following spring, Canadian troops dug up some remains, and the skull of the corpse believed to be al-Zawahiri was tested by the FBI. Forensic comparison of DNA, however, showed the skull was not al-Zawahiri's.

His whereabouts are currently unknown.

Glossary

Aga Khan: spiritual leader of the Ismaili Muslim movement

Allah: the Muslim god, or the Arabic name for God (still being debated by scholars)

Caliphate: the political embodiment of Islamic rule; the spiritual head and ruler of the Islamic state is the Caliph

Fatwa: religious ruling issued by an imam

Imam: Muslim religious leader

Islamist: militant Muslim who is politically motivated to actively pursue jihad

Jihad: Arabic word meaning "struggle," most often used to describe physical struggle in the cause of Allah; holy war (interpretive meaning)

Kurd: ethnic minority in northern Iraq and eastern Turkey

Mujahedin: Arabic word meaning "struggler," one who engages in jihad

Plenums: (in buildings) spaces for air circulation in air conditioning systems

Sharia: the Islamic way or path; a code of law

Shia: a branch of Islam, whose followers trace the political dynasty of their movement to Mohammed's cousin Ali, whom they say was nominated by Mohammed himself to succeed him

Shiite: adjective form of Shia

Sunni: a branch of Islam, whose followers trace the political dynasty of their movement to four caliphs (Islamic leader of the Muslim community; literally, "successor" of Mohammed. Various families have claimed the title over time, ending with the Ottomans) elected after Mohammed's death.

Sheik: (also spelled Sheikh) elder of an Arabic tribe, also used as title for men of stature in business or politics; traditional title of a Bedouin tribal leader.

Tawhid: recitation of the Koran with precise articulation and intonation

Note: Most words in the list have alternate spellings, as these are transliterations into English lettering of the sound of Arabic words. (What sounds like "mujahedin" to an American may sound like "mujehadin" or "mujahadeen" to other speakers of English.)

What Others Say

"The grooms are ready
for the big wedding."

*Attributed to Abu Zubaydah
prior to the attack on the
World Trade Center in 2001*

"We should like to inform the
Americans that, in short, their
message has been received and
that they should read carefully the
reply that will, with God's help,
be written in the language
that they understand."

Ayman al-Zawahiri, 1998

"A terrorist is someone who has a bomb,
but doesn't have an air force."

William Blum

"The Rewards For Justice Program, United States Department of State, is offering a reward of up to $25 million for information leading directly to the apprehension or conviction of Usama [Osama] Bin Laden. An additional $2 million is being offered through a program developed and funded by the Airline Pilots Association and the Air Transport Association.

From the FBI "Ten Most Wanted" web site

"The bomb left the embassy's ruined building as an eloquent and clear message."

Ayman al-Zawahiri after the 1995 bombing of the Egyptian Embassy in Islamabad, Pakistan

"Thank God. I performed jihad for 15 years until I earned this martyrdom."

Sayyid Qutb on being sentenced to death in 1966

"Any outlaw regime that has
ties to terrorist groups or seeks to
possess weapons of mass destruction
is a grave danger to the civilized
world and will be confronted."

President George W. Bush

"I'm absolutely convinced that
the threat we face now, the idea
of a terrorist in the middle of one
of our cities with a nuclear weapon,
is very real and that we have to use
extraordinary measures to deal with it."

Vice-president Dick Cheney

"Let me say this loud and clear. There is a
world of difference between terrorist acts
and the Islamic Shari'a. Islam is not only
a religion, but a way of life. And at its
heart lie the sacred principles of
tolerance and dialogue."

King Hussein

Select Bibliography

Bergen, Peter L. Holy War, Inc. *Inside the Secret World of Osama bin Laden.* The Free Press: New York, 2001.

Dyer, Joel. *Harvest of Rage: Why Oklahoma City is Only the Beginning.* Westview Press, a division of HarperCollins Publishers: Boulder, CO, 1997.

Lake, Anthony. *Nightmares.* Little, Brown and Company, Boston, MA, 2000.

Reeve, Simon. *The New Jackals: Ramzi Yousef, Osama bin Laden and the Future of Terrorism.* Northeastern University Press: Boston, MA, 1999.

Wright, Robin. *Sacred Rage: The Wrath of Militant Islam.* Simon & Shuster: New York, 1985.